Making Portfolios, Products, and Performances

Meaningful and Manageable for Students and Teachers

Instructional Strategies and Thematic Activities, Including a Pull-Out Graphic Organizer for Integrating Instruction

by Imogene Forte and Sandra Schurr

Incentive Publications, Inc.
Nashville, Tennessee

Cover and Illustrations by Geoffrey Brittingham
Edited by Leslie Britt and Karla Westerman

ISBN 0-86530-313-4

PRINTED IN THE UNITED STATES OF AMERICA

Table of Contents

Pull-Out Graphic Organizer For Integrating Instruction

PREFACE

Over the years, teachers have questioned the importance and appropriateness of using both standardized norm-referenced tests and traditional objective-based tests as the primary tools for measuring student achievement in the classroom. In many instances, the testing program itself has become the driving force behind curricular and instructional processes and has, in effect, limited the teacher's ability to teach and the student's motivation to learn.

Consequently, today's teachers and administrators continue to search for innovative ways to encourage student participation in the learning process and to utilize authentic measures to assess student growth in any given subject area. Authentic assessment is a more flexible and accurate type of evaluation than letter grades and pencil-paper tests because it requires the student to actively engage in the testing process and to provide evidence that genuine learning has taken place.

Authentic assessment tools and techniques have the following common characteristics:

1. An audience is required.

2. Few time constraints exist.

3. Collaboration is strongly encouraged.

4. Students participate in making decisions about the testing process.

5. A multi-faceted scoring system is used.

6. Student learning styles, interests, and ability levels are considered.

7. A self-assessment dimension is included.

8. Evaluation criteria is clearly presented before the task is assigned.

Teachers have found this to be a meaningful and achievable form of assessment, one especially dedicated to improving the communication that takes place in intermediate and middle grade classrooms. However, chief among the problems arising from the use of alternate assessment techniques has been a lack of common understanding among teachers, students, and parents of the criteria to be used in the preparation and evaluation stages and of how the activities ultimately relate to the students' long-range goals. While change always demands careful planning as well as a great deal of time and energy, it is especially important in the assessment process to establish clearly defined objectives so that the process proceeds in an orderly and mutually acceptable manner from its inception to its final form.

Making Portfolios, Products, and Performances Meaningful and Manageable for Students and Teachers has been written to help teachers sort out and make efficient use of these valuable approaches to evaluation. It provides both teachers and students with a wide variety of practical, effective options for enhancing the regular classroom routine and established instructional goals. The focus of the book is threefold: to provide activities that reveal the "how-to" aspects of 1) using portfolios to measure student growth 2) using products as potential artifacts in the portfolio and 3) using performances to share portfolio contents. Filled with high-interest pupil activities and easy-to-use record-keeping forms, each section also includes informative overviews and feedback forms for parents or guardians. Essentially, this research-based resource was developed to unite the home and school as collaborators in assessing student outcomes and making necessary instructional decisions.

Portfolios, products, and performances are the most widely recognized forms of authentic assessment in use today. Students enjoy the responsibility of selecting, preparing, and evaluating work to be included in their portfolios; developing products that are in keeping with specific evaluation criteria; and organizing performances that afford them a profound sense of ownership and a tremendous feeling of accomplishment.

Making
PORTFOLIOS
Meaningful
and
Manageable

A BIRD'S EYE VIEW OF STUDENT PORTFOLIOS

WHAT IS A PORTFOLIO?

A portfolio is a well-planned and organized collection of artifacts or selected pieces of student work. When used collaboratively by the student and the teacher, portfolios can monitor and measure the growth of a student's knowledge, skills, and attitudes in a specific subject area.

A BIRD'S EYE VIEW OF STUDENT PORTFOLIOS

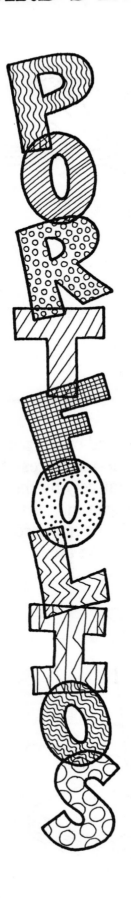

WHAT TYPES OF WORK SHOULD BE INCLUDED IN THE PORTFOLIO?

The portfolio should contain representative samples of student work, including such items as: homework tasks, quizzes and tests, learning logs, written work, survey/inventory results, self-assessment tools, independent and cooperative projects, video and audio tapes of performances, lab experiments, observation checklists, rough drafts of assignments, and completed individual and group products.

HOW SHOULD THE PORTFOLIO BE ORGANIZED?

The portfolio can be stored in a file box, notebook, or other appropriate container and should have these components:

(1) creative cover sheet that reflects interests and aptitudes of the student;

(2) table of contents that includes a list of portfolio items;

(3) student's written comments and reflections on the portfolio contents, including the reasons that specific pieces were selected;

(4) self-assessment of the portfolio by the student; and

(5) formal assessment of the portfolio by the teacher(s).

A BIRD'S EYE VIEW OF STUDENT PORTFOLIOS

HOW SHOULD THE PORTFOLIO BE GRADED OR EVALUATED?

Most pieces of work in the portfolio should be assessed throughout the duration of the class or course. Portfolio evaluation is, essentially, an ongoing process. For this reason, the portfolio itself is not usually assigned a formal grade, but instead contains many reflective comments by both the teacher and the student. In addition, a list of future goals based on the student's current needs and interests should be compiled and incorporated into the folder. In some instances, this valuable information and a few other selected items from the portfolio can be passed on to the next year's teacher.

WHO SELECTS THE PIECES FOR THE PORTFOLIO?

The portfolio should contain some pieces selected by the student and some pieces selected by the teacher. It is important to include some work samples that are "drafts" or "works in progress" as well as examples of finished products.

INTRODUCING AND SHARING PORTFOLIOS WITH YOUR FAMILY

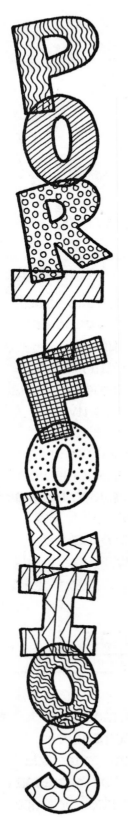

DIRECTIONS: (Step One)

It is important that your parents or guardians understand portfolios and their uses. Their support and involvement is an essential part of the portfolio process, from the planning stage through the assessment phase. Actually, your portfolio can become a very important tool for you to use to share projects, progress reports, and, most importantly, your feelings and experiences with your family. To accomplish this, you will want to make sure that your family members understand why your portfolio is being constructed, how it is being assembled, and what its major purposes are. Begin by carefully reading through the "Bird's Eye View" on pages 11-13 and discussing the information with your teachers and classmates to be sure you have a thorough understanding of what portfolios are all about. Now you are ready to share and explain the "Bird's Eye View" of portfolios to your parents or other important adults in your life.

INTRODUCING AND SHARING PORTFOLIOS WITH YOUR FAMILY

DIRECTIONS: (Step Two)

When your portfolio is complete, you will be taking it home to share with your family members. Their evaluation of your work is an important part of the whole portfolio experience. You will want to take the time to review with them the artifacts in your portfolio, explaining such things as why each item was chosen, what skills and concepts were applied, and how personal growth was achieved. In instances where the artifact was created as a result of a group effort, you will need to identify the other group members, explain your contribution to the project, and discuss the game plan and goals behind the activity. In presenting your portfolio, you will also want to refer to the criteria that was used by your teachers to give input in the developmental stages of your portfolio and to determine the overall quality of the completed task. Your family's feedback and suggestions can be extremely helpful in planning and constructing your next portfolio. For this reason, ask your family members to complete the Parent Portfolio Assessment Feedback Form (page 16) and return it to your teacher as promptly as possible.

PARENT PORTFOLIO ASSESSMENT FEEDBACK FORM

MY CHILD'S NAME _____ **DATE**_____

1. In your opinion, which piece reflects the most growth or progress of your child?

   _____

   _____

2. In your opinion, which piece best demonstrates your child's creative ability?

   _____

   _____

3. In your opinion, which piece shows the best evidence of application of thinking skills in your child's work?

   _____

   _____

4. In your opinion, which piece best shows the special interests and aptitudes of your child?

   _____

   _____

5. In your opinion, which piece best reflects your child's ability to read, research, write, or compute?

   _____

   _____

COMMENTS:

Signed_____

PORTFOLIO PLANNING SHEET

DIRECTIONS:

Use the outline below to record your ideas for developing a portfolio that will be reflective of your work in this course or subject area(s). Discuss your outline with other members of your class and with your teacher. Come to a group consensus on the look of the final portfolio.

1. List the major purpose of your portfolio.

_____

_____

2. List the types of pieces that you would include in your portfolio.

_____

_____

3. Explain how the pieces in the portfolio will be selected.

_____

_____

4. Describe how the contents of the portfolio will be organized.

_____

_____

5. Discuss how the contents of the portfolio will be assessed.

_____

_____

6. Summarize how the portfolio will be shared with others—peers, parents, and next year's teacher.

_____

_____

Name _____ Date _____

MY PLAN FOR A PORTFOLIO IN

_____

(List Subject)

I would like to create a portfolio that shows my growth in the above subject area. The ten pieces I would like to include in my portfolio are:

1. _____
2. _____
3. _____
4. _____
5. _____
6. _____
7. _____
8. _____
9. _____
10. _____

I would like my portfolio to be evaluated in the following way:
(Check all that apply.)

_____1. Each piece in the portfolio is graded separately, and there is no single grade for the portfolio itself.

_____2. The entire portfolio is given an overall grade that reflects a given set of criteria established jointly by the student and teacher.

_____3. No grade is given for either the portfolio as a whole or the individual pieces within the portfolio because the portfolio pieces are only representative of the student's ability over a predetermined period of time.

_____4. Each piece within the portfolio is given a specific grade, and a final grade is also given for the overall contents and organization of the portfolio.

_____5. A rubric is developed for the portfolio content which is used to assess the individual pieces within the portfolio.

Name _____ Date _____

CREATING A MOCK PORTFOLIO

DIRECTIONS:

Review the list of artifacts below that one might include in a portfolio for any course or class. Then, pretend you are the teacher and write on a separate sheet of paper at least ten items that you would require your students to include in their portfolios for your class. Be specific in your descriptions. For example, if you were creating a portfolio in math, you might want to include such items as a mathematical autobiography, a series of word problems you made up with their correct solutions, and a math quiz on fractions.

POSSIBLE ARTIFACTS FOR ANY TYPE OF PORTFOLIO IN ANY SUBJECT AREA:

1. Research or investigative reports
2. Responses to open-ended questions or starter statements
3. Group worksheets and photographs of group projects
4. Copies of awards or prizes
5. Video tapes, audio tapes, or computer-generated examples of student's work
6. Homework papers
7. Learning or problem-solving logs
8. Teacher-made tests and quizzes
9. Written work
10. Reflective journals or diaries
11. Textbook assignments
12. Rough drafts or works in progress
13. Personal surveys, questionnaires, or inventories
14. Interview or conference results
15. Observation checklists or anecdotal records
16. Laboratory experiments
17. Self-assessments
18. Peer assessments
19. Photographs, audio tapes, or video tapes of speeches, plays, debates, role plays, panels, exhibits, demonstrations, or presentations
20. Metacognitive activities
21. Drawings, diagrams, charts, graphs, or flow charts
22. Samples of artwork
23. Creative writing pieces and thinking tasks
24. Graphic organizers
25. Corrections to missed problems, questions, or assigned tasks

DIRECTIONS:

You will be creating a mini-portfolio all about YOU. This portfolio activity will help you understand what a portfolio is and how it is put together. To complete this activity, select any ten artifacts from the list on page 21 to complete and include in your portfolio. Before you begin this activity, be sure you have designed your portfolio container (a box, notebook, file folder, scrapbook, etc.) and have decided the manner in which you will share your portfolio contents with others (display, presentation, video, etc.).

Read through the list of possible artifacts and select the ones that you think will be most appropriate for your "ME" portfolio. Then use words and sketches to develop a plan of action for organizing your own portfolio.

POSSIBLE ARTIFACTS FOR YOUR "ME" PORTFOLIO

____1. Name poem using your first and last names (Each letter in your name is used to begin a phrase that describes something about you.)

____2. Timeline of the most important events in your life to date

____3. Autobiography (no more than three pages)

____4. Photo essay about a special interest or hobby

____5. Description of your most prized possession

____6. Bookmark describing your favorite novel

____7. How-to speech on a personal hobby or interest

____8. Series of diary entries on your personal thoughts and/or daily events

____9. Mock invitation or greeting card you would like to receive

___10. Editorial for the school/local newspaper on a subject about which you feel strongly

___11. Audio tape of your favorite music with a brief explanation of your choices

___12. Collection of your favorite proverbs or quotations

___13. Poster or collage of things that are important to you

___14. Interview you conduct with a special adult

___15. Circle graph of your perfect day

___16. Piece of art or sculpture you have created

___17. Self-portrait

___18. Perfect horoscope for a day

___19. Award you would like to receive

___20. Other (to be determined by you)

CHECK ALL OF THE ARTIFACTS THAT APPLY TO YOU.

Name _____ Date _____

YOU ARE THE TEACHER!

DIRECTIONS:

Pretend you are the teacher in each of the following subject areas. You want your students to keep a portfolio for the semester. Review the list of suggested artifacts for each topic and add additional requirements of your own on the blank lines provided. Be creative in your thinking and planning. Include items which you would be interested in developing if you were the student!

POSSIBLE ARTIFACTS FOR POETRY PORTFOLIOS
ENGLISH/LANGUAGE ARTS CLASS

- Bibliography of poetry books written especially for kids
- Review of one poetry book from your bibliography
- Illustration to accompany a favorite poem by a favorite poet
- Glossary of poetry terms
- Biography of a famous poet
- Original haiku, diamante, limerick, or tanka poem

_____

_____

_____

_____

_____

_____

_____

_____

_____

_____

Name _____ Date _____

POSSIBLE ARTIFACTS FOR GEOGRAPHY PORTFOLIO

SOCIAL STUDIES CLASS

- Sample objective test from geography unit
- Cooperative learning activity: "Invent a Country"
- Samples of student-created world maps
- Papier-mâché globe
- Researched report of a country
- Chart comparing continents of the world

_____

_____

_____

_____

_____

_____

_____

_____

_____

_____

_____

_____

_____

_____

_____

Name _____ Date _____

POSSIBLE ARTIFACTS FOR PORTFOLIO
ON ROCKS AND MINERALS

SCIENCE CLASS

- Diagram of igneous, metamorphic, and sedimentary rock formations
- Lab report of classroom experiment on limestone
- Creative writing samples: "Obituary of a Rock"
- Rock collection with correct labels
- Results of your interview with a "Rock Hound"
- Creation of a pet rock and directions for its care

Name _____ Date _____

POSSIBLE ARTIFACTS FOR PORTFOLIO
ON FRACTIONS

MATH CLASS

- Sample problems/answers from end-of-chapter textbook lesson
- Results of classroom fraction treasure hunt
- Collage of fractions from the newspaper
- Chart showing how to compute number operations with fractions
- Report: "Without Fractions, Everything Would Be All Or Nothing"
- Your design of a math game about fractions

Name _____ Date _____

USING A THEMATIC MINI-UNIT
WITH A SCIENCE FOCUS
TO DEVELOP A PORTFOLIO ARTIFACT

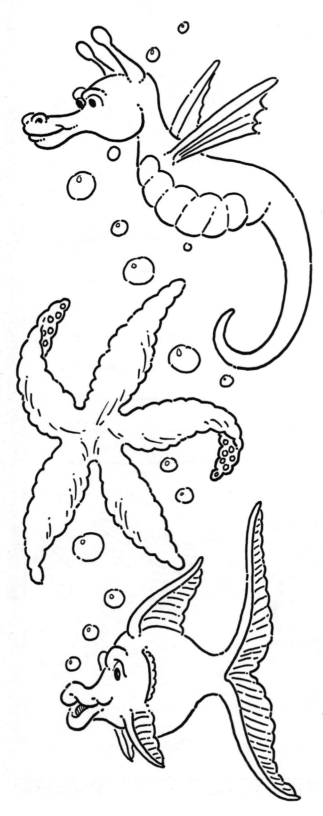

Directions:

Creatures of the Deep is a thematic mini-unit that has been developed according to Bloom's Taxonomy to help you reinforce and/or extend basic science concepts, use critical thinking skills, and learn some interesting facts about ocean animals. After you have completed all of the activities according to the directions, select one piece of work to add to your portfolio. Just for your own information, check at least three criteria on page 27 that you used for selecting this particular piece of work to add to your portfolio. Then check one item in each of the other two categories that best describes your feelings about the assignment.

CREATURES OF THE DEEP

I am selecting this piece for my portfolio based on . . . (choose three)

_____ neatness
_____ creativity
_____ accuracy
_____ originality
_____ thoroughness
_____ interesting content

_____ other_____

_____

_____

On the whole, I found this assignment to be . . . (choose one and explain)

_____ boring
_____ relatively interesting
_____ interesting
_____ very interesting

because _____

_____

_____

**Now that I know more about ocean animals than I did before,
I would like to . . .** (choose one)

_____ learn more about them
_____ take a field trip to an aquarium to observe ocean animals
_____ research and write a detailed report on one particular animal whose
natural habitat is the ocean

_____ other_____

_____

_____

Name_____ Date _____

CREATURES OF THE DEEP

Knowledge:
List the names of ten animals whose natural habitat is the ocean. Give one important characteristic of each animal.

Comprehension:
Outline a plan for educating the world's human population about protection of the ocean's endangered animal species.

Application:
Predict the effects of sewage and waste dumping on ocean life over the next ten years if the disposal continues at the present rate. Design a bar graph to show your predictions.

Synthesis:
Select body parts of 5 different ocean animals to create a new animal. Use modeling clay to make a model of the animal, or draw a picture of the animal, give it a name, and list its special features and habits.

Analysis:
Finish the following comparisons with appropriate ocean animal names.

As wild as a(an)_____.

As playful and friendly as a(an)_____.

As huge as a(an)_____.

As colorful as a(an)_____.

As dangerous as a(an)_____.

Create three comparisons of your own.

Evaluation:
Pretend that you are going to contribute money to help educate students your own age about the animals of the ocean. Determine which of the following programs you would support. Justify your decision with three good reasons.

(A) Production of a documentary video on ocean animals, their habitats, and their contributions to the world's economy.

(B) Construction and maintenance of a first-class aquarium.

(C) Development of a textbook series, complete with teachers' manuals and student workbooks, dedicated to the study of ocean animals.

©1995 by Incentive Publications, Inc., Nashville, TN.

USING INVESTIGATION CARDS
WITH A SOCIAL STUDIES FOCUS
TO DEVELOP A PORTFOLIO ARTIFACT

DIRECTIONS:

Investigate Our National Parks is a set of investigation cards that has been developed according to Bloom's Taxonomy to help you extend and make meaningful use of social studies concepts and critical thinking skills.

After you have completed at least one card from each level of Bloom's Taxonomy (Knowledge, Comprehension, Application, Analysis, Synthesis, and Evaluation), select one piece of work to add to your portfolio.

In the space below give the reasons for and criteria of your selection.

I selected this particular piece of work for my portfolio because

_____

_____

_____

_____

_____

I evaluated this piece of work in terms of its _____

_____

_____

_____

Name _____ Date _____

SOCIAL STUDIES

INVESTIGATE OUR
NATIONAL PARKS

SOCIAL STUDIES

INVESTIGATE OUR
NATIONAL PARKS

SOCIAL STUDIES

INVESTIGATE OUR
NATIONAL PARKS

SOCIAL STUDIES

INVESTIGATE OUR
NATIONAL PARKS

SOCIAL STUDIES

INVESTIGATE OUR
NATIONAL PARKS

SOCIAL STUDIES

INVESTIGATE OUR
NATIONAL PARKS

List as many of our country's
national parks as you can.

KNOWLEDGE

In your own words, explain why
national parks were created.

COMPREHENSION

Define:
national park,
national monument,
historical site

KNOWLEDGE

Describe some environmental
dangers that are threatening
the survival of our most
popular national parks.

COMPREHENSION

Record the types of things
a person would expect to see and do
at a typical national park.

KNOWLEDGE

Summarize why
visits to national parks
are so popular with tourists.

COMPREHENSION

Research to find out about at least twenty of our national parks. Then construct a set of Fact Cards about each one that tells:
1. its name and location;
2. its area in square miles; and
3. its special features.

APPLICATION

Compare and contrast any two of our national parks from diverse parts of the country.

ANALYSIS

Write a set of high-quality questions that you would like to ask a park ranger about his or her job.

APPLICATION

Draw conclusions about the type of vacationer that is most likely to visit a national park.

ANALYSIS

Construct a timeline to mark the history of our national park system, from its beginnings to the present.

APPLICATION

Debate the advantages of visiting a national park with those of visiting a commercially-developed national tourist attraction.

ANALYSIS

Invent a new national park.
Give it a name. Describe its size,
location, and special features.

SYNTHESIS

Rank the following states according
to the number and quality of the
national parks contained within their
borders, with 1 being the most
desirable and 4 being the least
desirable. The states to consider are:
Utah, California, Alaska, and Arizona.

EVALUATION

Create a set of color postcards showing
several scenes from your new
national park. Consider pictures
of lakes, meadows, mountains,
wildflowers, wildlife,
recreational facilities, etc.

SYNTHESIS

Critique the contributions of the
following organizations to the
development and protection of
our country's national parks:
U.S. Department of the Interior,
Sierra Club, Wilderness Society,
and the Audubon Society.

EVALUATION

Design an attractive travel brochure to
advertise and promote visitors to your
new national park.

SYNTHESIS

Determine which of the following activities
would be most popular with students in
your class if they were selecting national
parks to visit on a summer tour: hiking,
camping, backpacking, birdwatching,
horseback riding, fishing, river rafting,
bicycling, kayaking or canoeing, cave
exploring, or mountain climbing.
Be able to justify your choices.

EVALUATION

USING JOURNAL ENTRIES OR LEARNING LOGS AS PORTFOLIO ARTIFACTS

DIRECTIONS:

Keeping a journal in a given course or subject area can be very useful as part of the authentic assessment process. Journals help us to improve our writing skills, thinking skills, reflective skills, metacognitive skills, and test-taking skills. When used as an integral part of the classroom experience, journals become information sources for class discussions, study sessions prior to tests and quizzes, brainstorming activities, problem-solving situations, and for the communication of innermost thoughts, feelings, or reactions. Simply stated, journals and learning logs are personal records of information sought and insights gained and are the property of the writer.

SOME TYPES OF INFORMATION TO BE RECORDED IN MY JOURNAL:

1. Key points from a lecture, audiovisual presentation, experiment, class demonstration, or textbook assignment

2. Questions generated from a discussion, research, or reading task

3. Summaries of main ideas from a lecture, audiovisual presentation, experiment, class demonstration, or textbook assignment

4. Responses to questions or challenges posed by the teacher or peers

5. Reflections on subject matter, controversial issues, or points to ponder

6. Results of brainstorming and problem-solving sessions

7. Timelines and progress reports of ongoing projects

8. Connections between related pieces of information from varied subject areas

9. Random thoughts and reactions to ideas, innovations, and assignments

10. Goals, hopes, dreams, and plans for the future

GENERIC WRITING PROMPTS TO RECORD CLASSROOM LEARNING

DIRECTIONS:

The following writing prompts may be entered into your journal or learning log and used to record your ideas on topics currently being studied in class.

1. Today in class I learned . . .

2. I was surprised to know that . . .

3. I discovered an important fact which is . . .

4. I was pleased to find out that . . .

5. What I like most or least about this topic is . . .

6. I think I should spend more time finding out . . .

7. If I could share one thing about today's lesson, it would be . . .

8. I wish I didn't have to know . . .

9. I was pleased that I . . .

10. I would never want to . . .

11. The most difficult part of this lesson to understand was . . .

12. The easiest part of this lesson to understand was . . .

13. When I find or figure out an answer I feel . . .

14. What I still don't understand is . . .

15. Of the work we've done lately, I'm most confident about . . .

16. Some new questions this work raised are . . .

17. My plan for what I will do tomorrow is . . .

GENERIC WRITING PROMPTS TO ASSESS CONTENT-AREA LEARNING

DIRECTIONS:

The following writing prompts can be entered into your journal or learning log and used to record your ideas on topics currently being studied in class. Choose one or more to complete about a specific lesson you participated in today.

1. Summarize in your own words the meaning of . . .

2. Discuss what is most important to know about . . .

3. How would you explain . . . to a student who doesn't understand?

4. Explain your reasoning about . . .

5. Describe the images that come to mind when you think about . . .

6. As part of the group assignment, it was my job to . . .

7. I can relate what I learned today to . . .

8. To make my group work better, I could have . . .

9. To make this lesson more productive and meaningful, I could have . . .

10. The questions that I would like answered in tomorrow's lesson are . . .

WRITING PROMPTS TO STRETCH YOUR MIND AND TEASE YOUR IMAGINATION

DIRECTIONS:

Choose one of the following writing prompts to complete in your journal or learning log:

1. Write a letter to your parents explaining what you learned in class today. Include specific details about the topic that you think would be of interest to them.

2. Write a reflective essay explaining to others how you have felt over the years and how you feel now about one of the following subjects: math, science, social studies, or language arts. Discuss situations and activities that have been successful for you in that area as well as problems you have experienced. Describe the "best" and the "worst" types of assignments you have encountered as part of the course.

3. Write an editorial to your school newspaper stating your opinion about the way this subject is taught.

4. Draw a picture, diagram, or flow chart to illustrate something you learned in class today.

5. Design two billboards about today's lesson, one humorous and one serious.

6. Create an editorial cartoon illustrating some aspect of today's classroom activities.

SAMPLE CONTENT-AREA WRITING PROMPTS

DIRECTIONS:

On pages 38-41 are sample writing prompts for four different topics that could be used to stimulate reflective thoughts to be recorded in personal learning logs or journals. Read them carefully and think about how you could use them as aids to your own journal writing. Then add some starter statements or questions of your own.

SOCIAL STUDIES: Writing Prompts for a Study of Consumerism

1. What do you already know about good consumer buying and spending habits?
2. What do you want to know about making wise choices with your money?
3. Do you get an allowance? If so, how much, and what do you have to do to earn it?
4. What makes a "good buy" or "bargain" for you?
5. What do you spend most of your money on?
6. Do you think kids should be paid for going to school? Explain.
7. What is the most expensive thing you have ever bought with your own money? Did you get your money's worth?
8. What is a budget, and how can it be helpful to a consumer?
9. Why should people save money? Why do you think some people find it difficult to save money?
10. Think about the many jobs that people have in our country today and the kinds of salaries they earn. Consider entertainers, athletes, doctors, lawyers, teachers, postal workers, policemen, computer technicians, custodians, waitresses, retail clerks, and airline pilots. Do you think people deserve what they earn? Explain.

Now . . . add some of your own!

_____

_____

_____

_____

_____

_____

Name _____ Date _____

SCIENCE: Writing Prompts for a Study of Weather

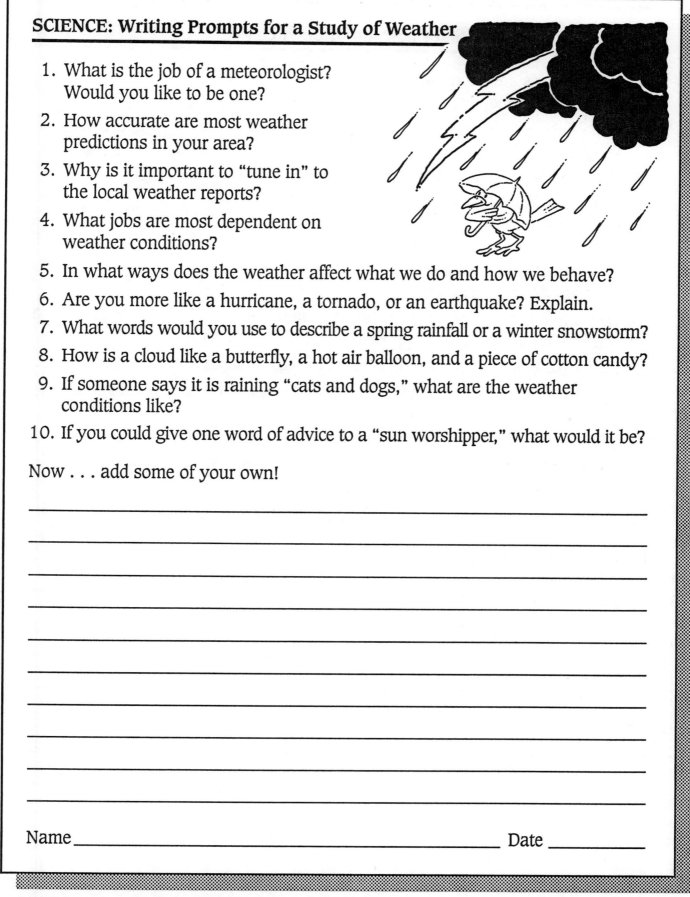

1. What is the job of a meteorologist? Would you like to be one?

2. How accurate are most weather predictions in your area?

3. Why is it important to "tune in" to the local weather reports?

4. What jobs are most dependent on weather conditions?

5. In what ways does the weather affect what we do and how we behave?

6. Are you more like a hurricane, a tornado, or an earthquake? Explain.

7. What words would you use to describe a spring rainfall or a winter snowstorm?

8. How is a cloud like a butterfly, a hot air balloon, and a piece of cotton candy?

9. If someone says it is raining "cats and dogs," what are the weather conditions like?

10. If you could give one word of advice to a "sun worshipper," what would it be?

Now . . . add some of your own!

_____

_____

_____

_____

_____

_____

_____

_____

_____

_____

Name _____ Date _____

MATH: Writing Prompts for a Study of Geometry

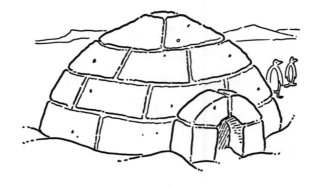

1. What shapes are important in a house, tent, igloo, and houseboat?

2. Why do structures stand up?

3. What evidence of geometrical shapes do you find in nature?

4. What seems to be the most common shape in your classroom? Give examples to support your hypothesis.

5. Name five geometrical shapes and give examples of how they are used in an artificial environment (as opposed to a natural environment).

6. Sketch a dwelling made solely from either hexagons, trapezoids, circles, or triangles.

7. What would it feel like to be an artist like Picasso who used vivid geometric figures in his work?

8. Explain each of these figurative expressions: (1) She is always running around in circles; (2) He is so square; (3) They know all the angles.

9. A good way to determine the area of a room is . . .

10. What is the relationship of geometry to the world of fashion?

Now . . . add some of your own!

_____

_____

_____

_____

_____

_____

_____

Name _____ Date _____

LANGUAGE ARTS: Writing Prompts for a Study of Grammar

1. Explain why grammar is important to a student, an author, a newspaper reporter, and a television reporter.

2. Why do some kids dislike grammar?

3. What was the hardest thing for you to learn about sentence structure?

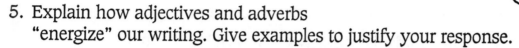

4. Make a list of your favorite nouns and verbs. Write a good paragraph that includes most of them.

5. Explain how adjectives and adverbs "energize" our writing. Give examples to justify your response.

6. If you were to give one piece of advice to a foreign student trying to learn English, what would it be?

7. Give five reasons why it is important to learn the parts of speech.

8. Explain the difference between a subject and a predicate.

9. List at least three questions that you have about our grammar lesson today. Record at least three things you learned from today's lesson.

10. Are you more like a comma, an exclamation point, a question mark, or a period? Explain.

Now . . . add some of your own!

_____

_____

_____

_____

_____

_____

_____

Name_____ Date _____

WRITING GOOD TEST QUESTIONS AS PART OF THE PORTFOLIO PROCESS

DIRECTIONS:

Paper-and-pencil tests can be useful artifacts for a portfolio if they are clear, concise, and fair. Some basic rules for writing good objective test items are listed below. Review these guidelines. Then, select a topic of interest to you and write one good question for each category following the suggested guidelines. Complete this activity on a separate sheet of paper and be sure to include your answers to the questions you have created.

TRUE/FALSE GUIDELINES

1. Make each item focused on one idea or concept.

2. Avoid absolute words like "always," "never," and "only."

3. State each item in a positive fashion.

4. Make each item either clearly true or clearly false.

5. Limit the number of test items to ten and make all test items approximately the same number of words in length.

Bonus: Consider asking the students to make false questions true for extra credit or practice.

MULTIPLE CHOICE GUIDELINES

1. Make the stem of the question brief and based on the main idea.

2. Make incorrect choices feasible and/or reasonable possibilities.

3. Make stems of equal length and their alternatives of equal length.

4. Arrange alternative responses in random sequence and avoid using such choices as "none of the above" or "all of the above."

5. Use correct grammar and punctuation between stems and their corresponding alternatives.

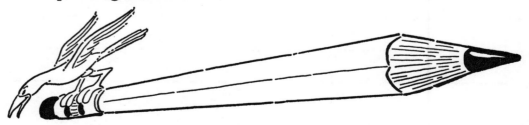

WRITING GOOD TEST QUESTIONS AS PART OF THE PORTFOLIO PROCESS

MATCHING GUIDELINES

1. Include more choices than initial questions and statements.

2. Limit list of matching items to no more than ten and no less than five.

3. Make certain that items are similar in content and that you do not mix up names, places, dates, events, and things.

COMPLETION GUIDELINES

1. Design each item to require a brief and specific answer.

2. Use blanks of equal length.

3. Use only one blank in each statement.

4. Do not use ambiguous statements that could have more than one correct response.

5. Avoid direct statements or passages from a textbook.

ESSAY GUIDELINES

1. Write questions that require higher-order thinking skills rather than memorization of facts.

2. Design questions that outline a specific task or tasks that can be completed in a reasonable period of time.

3. Write questions that require information from the student upon which most teachers would agree as being correct or complete.

4. Define criteria (checklist of informational points) and assign point values for each question.

5. Avoid use of optional questions or opinion questions that can lead students away from the major concepts of the test.

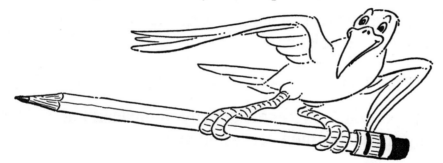

CREATING A RUBRIC FOR EVALUATING MY PORTFOLIO

DIRECTIONS:

A rubric is a description of evaluation standards or a list of criteria to be used in determining the quality of an assignment, task, or product. A sample rubric for student portfolios begins below and continues on pages 45 and 46. Study the rubric, then design one for yourself on a separate sheet of paper that could be used to assess a portfolio that you created for a given course or subject area.

EXCELLENT

CHARACTERISTICS:

1. My portfolio is complete.

2. My portfolio is organized.

3. My portfolio is visually exciting.

4. My portfolio contains many varied samples of written work.

5. My portfolio shows much evidence of using multiple resources.

6. My portfolio shows much evidence of problem-solving, decision-making, and practice of thinking skills.

7. My portfolio includes many samples of individual and group work.

8. My portfolio includes many self-assessment tools and reflective comments.

9. My portfolio reflects my enthusiasm for the subject.

10. My portfolio contains many additional pieces that were not required or assigned.

11. My portfolio communicates effectively what I have learned.

12. My portfolio has identified many future learning goals to meet my special learning needs and interests.

GOOD

CHARACTERISTICS:

1. My portfolio is complete.

2. My portfolio is organized.

3. My portfolio is interesting.

4. My portfolio contains several examples of written work.

5. My portfolio shows some evidence of using multiple resources.

6. My portfolio shows some evidence of problem-solving, decision-making, and practice of thinking skills.

7. My portfolio includes some examples of individual and group work.

8. My portfolio includes some examples of self-assessment tools and reflective comments.

9. My portfolio reflects some interest for the subject.

10. My portfolio contains some additional pieces that were not required or assigned.

11. My portfolio communicates some things that I have learned.

12. My portfolio has identified some future learning goals to meet my special learning needs and interests.

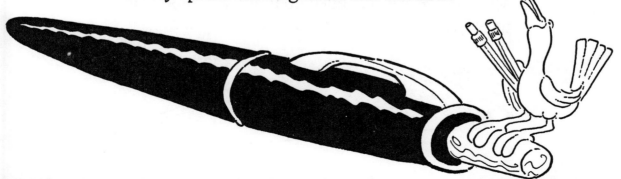

NEEDS
IMPROVEMENT

CHARACTERISTICS:

1. My portfolio is incomplete.

2. My portfolio is unorganized.

3. My portfolio is not very interesting to others.

4. My portfolio contains few examples of written work.

5. My portfolio shows little evidence of using multiple resources.

6. My portfolio shows little evidence of problem-solving, decision-making, and practice of thinking skills.

7. My portfolio includes few examples of individual and group work.

8. My portfolio includes few examples of self-assessment tools and reflective comments.

9. My portfolio reflects little interest for the subject.

10. My portfolio contains no additional pieces that were not required or assigned.

11. My portfolio communicates few things that I have learned.

12. My portfolio has identified no future learning goals to meet my special learning needs and interests.

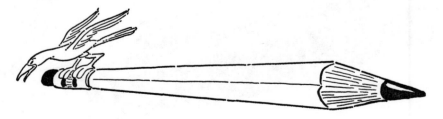

A DO-IT-YOURSELF RUBRIC FOR PORTFOLIOS

DIRECTIONS:

Use this blank form to create a holistic or analytic rubric for evaluating a portfolio. A holistic rubric assigns levels of performance with descriptors for each level, while an analytic rubric assigns levels of performance with numerical points allocated for every descriptor at each level.

TOP LEVELS

Descriptors   Points Awarded

_____   _____

_____   _____

_____   _____

MEDIUM LEVELS

Descriptors   Points Awarded

_____   _____

_____   _____

_____   _____

LOW LEVELS

Descriptors   Points Awarded

_____   _____

_____   _____

_____   _____

NOTE: You can add as many levels as you want and as many descriptors as you want. You can also create your own labels for the levels and use such categories as: Exemplary Achievement, Commendable Achievement, Limited Evidence of Achievement, and Minimal Achievement.

Name _____ Date _____

PERSONAL REFLECTIONS ABOUT MY PORTFOLIO

DIRECTIONS:

Look through the artifacts in your portfolio and arrange them in some type of order—by date, by topic, by preference, or by quality of results. Take time to review these pieces and reflect upon the growth or changes you see in them over a period of time. Ask yourself such questions as:

(1) What can I do now that I couldn't do before?

(2) What do I know now that I didn't know before?

(3) What things can I do better?

(4) In what areas do I still need to make improvements?

(5) What could I do differently next time?

(6) What tasks represented in the portfolio were easiest for me to do? Most difficult for me to do? Most interesting and fun for me to do?

Next, use the space below to write a "reflective essay" on your progress as represented by the work in this portfolio. Use another piece of paper if you need more room for your reflections.

Name _____ Date _____

Making
PRODUCTS
Meaningful
and
Manageable

WHAT IS PRODUCT ASSESSMENT?

Student products are work that students have generated or created. It is important that students help establish the assignment guidelines and be allowed to make many of their own decisions when engaging in product development. This empowers them with a considerable amount of ownership in the assessment process.

A BIRD'S EYE VIEW OF STUDENT PRODUCTS

WHY IS PRODUCT ASSESSMENT DESIRABLE?

Student products are valuable evaluation tools because they:

(1) give students an opportunity to show their creativity and knowledge base which often goes beyond what has been formally taught;

(2) demonstrate student growth in both academic skills and independent work habits that will not be reflected in standardized tests; and

(3) foster decision-making and problem-solving skills as students assume responsibility for making product choices and sticking to established timelines and action plans.

WHAT ARE SOME ADVANTAGES OF PRODUCT ASSESSMENT FOR THE STUDENT?

Product assessment helps to:

(1) motivate the student who typically lacks enthusiasm because projects are often more stimulating and are more directly related to the real world;

(2) give students more ownership of what and how they learn;

(3) encourage students to interact and collaborate with one another and to be more flexible and open in group situations.

A BIRD'S EYE VIEW OF STUDENT PRODUCTS

WHAT ARE SOME COMMON TYPES OF PRODUCTS?

Products are limited only by a student's imagination and creativity. Products may include anything from the physical construction of art items such as models, dioramas, and mobiles to investigative reports, video tapes, inventions, and interviews.

HOW SHOULD PRODUCTS BE EVALUATED?

Although these will vary from product to product and teacher to teacher, the general guidelines are as follows:

(1) Criteria for evaluation will be established before products are started and will include student input.

(2) Grades will reflect both numerical ratings and personal comments/ observations/recommendations.

(3) Products will become part of the portfolio requirements.

(4) Students will be assessed on both the process of product development and the end result of the product itself.

INTRODUCING AND SHARING PRODUCT ASSESSMENT WITH YOUR FAMILY

DIRECTIONS: (Step One)

When members of your family and/or other important adults in your life know about and understand how product assessment works, the products themselves, as well as the procedures you use in their completion, take on a whole new meaning for them and for you. When you inform and involve your family members in the planning and development of the product, they will have a better understanding of the assessment criteria, will be better able to determine your progress, and can assist you with preparing for future projects. Actually, this can also become a meaningful and effective channel for sharing personal experiences and feelings with your family. To accomplish this, you will want to make sure your family members understand how and why each product is being constructed, what its major purposes are, and how it will be evaluated. Begin by carefully reading through the "Bird's Eye View" on pages 51-53 and discussing it with your teachers and classmates to be sure you have a thorough understanding of what products are all about. Now you are ready to share and explain the "Bird's Eye View" of products to your parents and/or other important adults in your life.

INTRODUCING AND SHARING PRODUCT ASSESSMENT WITH YOUR FAMILY

DIRECTIONS: (Step Two)

When your product is complete, you will be taking it home to share with your family members. Their evaluation of your work is an important part of the entire learning experience. Take the time to review the product with them in great detail, explaining such things as why the topic or theme was chosen, how each step contributed to the development of the product, and what criteria was used to evaluate your work. Discuss your perception of personal growth as a result of the project. In instances where the product was created as a result of a group effort, you will need to identify the other group members, explain your contribution to the project, and discuss the game plan and goals behind the activity. In presenting your product, list the criteria used by your teachers to guide the development of the product as well as to determine its final assessment. Your family's feedback and suggestions can be extremely helpful in planning and constructing your next product. For this reason, ask your family members to complete the Parent Product Assessment Feedback Form (page 56) and return it to your teacher as promptly as possible.

PARENT PRODUCT ASSESSMENT FEEDBACK FORM

MY CHILD'S NAME _____ **DATE**_____

FAMILY MEMBERS PRESENT FOR PRODUCT ASSESSMENT EXPLANATION:

_____

_____

1. What was your initial reaction to the idea of product assessment in our classroom?

   _____

2. Do you remember creating student products such as book reports, dioramas, posters, and other projects? If so, how did you feel about them? If not, would you have liked creating such products?

   _____

3. What do you feel are the advantages and disadvantages of product development for your child?

   _____

4. Has your child created projects in school for other classes over the years? If so, how successful do you feel these projects were in helping you to better understand your child's social and/or academic progress?

   _____

5. How might family members get involved in or assist your child with the development of projects as part of his or her assessment process?

   _____

6. In general, do you feel that product assessment is a good approach to evaluating your child's progress in school?

   _____

COMMENTS:

Signed_____

STUDENT PRODUCT PLANNING FORM

DIRECTIONS:

This form provides an outline for planning a high-quality project/product. Use this tool to help design your project so that you have a "plan of action" for getting the job done right!

NAME_____ CLASS/COURSE _____

BEGINNING DATE OF PROJECT_____ COMPLETION DATE OF PROJECT _____

PROJECT TOPIC_____

PROJECT FORMAT _____

GUIDING QUESTIONS TO BE ANSWERED IN MY PROJECT:

_____

_____

_____

DATA SOURCES TO BE USED IN RESEARCH FOR MY PROJECT: (Check all that apply.)

_____ Factual books   _____ Surveys or questionnaires

_____ Interviews   _____ Letters requesting information

_____ Audiovisual resources _____ Newspapers and magazines

_____ Experiments   _____ Other (please specify)_____

PROBLEMS I MAY ENCOUNTER IN COMPLETING MY PROJECT:

_____

_____

_____

ASSISTANCE I WILL NEED FROM OTHERS IN COMPLETING MY PROJECT:

_____

_____

CRITERIA TO BE USED IN EVALUATING MY PROJECT:

_____

_____

GRADE I EXPECT TO RECEIVE ON MY PROJECT: _____

TWENTY-FIVE SPRINGBOARDS FOR PRODUCT INVESTIGATIONS AND PROCESSES BY STUDENTS

It is important that any project you do is manageable in terms of time, energy, resources, and information to be presented. For this reason, you should limit the number of big questions to answer, big ideas to research, or big objectives to cover. One way to do this is to choose a key behavior, or verb, as the basis for your project. It is important, however, to be wise and cautious as you select the words to define what you will be doing or making. Some sample springboards are listed below. Use the examples as future project ideas, or refer to them as models for developing your own unique springboards.

1. **Compare** and **contrast** _____ with _____, discussing their similarities and differences.

2. **Define** and **explain** the relationship between _____ and _____ .

3. **Develop** a reasonable hypothesis about something. Then devise a test, experiment, or survey to prove or disprove your hypothesis.

4. **Construct** a model to appraise something. Label the parts, and create a diagram to show how it works.

5. **Create** a survey or questionnaire to measure outside attitudes, positions, knowledge, or sentiments about a controversial issue. Interpret and publish the results.

6. **Observe** some people, places, or things. Record what you see. Make inferences or draw conclusions about your observations.

7. **Combine** two or more ideas/elements/concepts to make a new one.

8. **Develop** your own theory or philosophy about something.

9. **Perform** a controlled experiment. Summarize the results and make predictions about future results.

10. **Develop** a classification scheme. Divide things into categories. Determine appropriate divisions and descriptive labels.

TWENTY-FIVE SPRINGBOARDS FOR PRODUCT INVESTIGATIONS AND PROCESSES BY STUDENTS

11. **Identify** a problem and **pose** several alternative solutions. Decide on the best solution and think of ways to promote it.

12. **Ask** a series of "what if" questions and try to answer them.

13. **Develop** your own definitions and applications for important terms or concepts.

14. **Determine** the causes and effects of selected events.

15. **Analyze** a situation or an object. Break it down into its component parts. Find out about the parts and how they work or function.

16. **Conduct** an "implication" study. What implications does a specific decision, behavior, or attitude have on a group of people?

17. **Cite** facts and opinions on a given topic or issue. Distinguish between the two.

18. **Transfer** characters, events, or ideas to another time zone, culture, or historical period and describe the effects.

19. **View** an incident or experience from different and varied perspectives.

20. **Select** an issue and **outline** the pros and cons or the advantages and disadvantages of the issue.

21. **Identify** a trend and think of ways to measure its effect, influence, growth, or decline.

22. **Identify** a structure and **illustrate** how it functions.

23. **Take** a position on an issue and find ways to prove that you are right.

24. **Examine** various types of data or data sources and **rank** them in some meaningful way or make generalizations about them.

25. **Rearrange** words, parts, or positions of something to create a new and different whole.

CREATIVE SPRINGBOARDS FOR
STUDENT-GENERATED PROJECTS

1. BOOKMARKS AND BOOK PLATES:

Create a set of related bookmarks or book plates based on a theme or topic. The bookmarks may contain a set of facts on one side and a descriptive paragraph or diagram on the other side. The book plates may contain summaries of important ideas or samples of original work.
Examples:

- A set of nine bookmarks on the Solar System, with one bookmark for each planet
- A set of five book plates on poetry forms (haiku, limerick, tanka, free verse, and diamante), with original poems

2. DISCOVERY PLACE MATS:

Design a set of related discovery place mats based on a theme or topic. The place mats may be drawn on posterboard or heavy construction paper and laminated for durability. Each place mat should feature a collection of important facts, definitions, and graphics in a given content area that could be used as a study guide while eating lunch at school or dinner at home. The place mats may even include simple quizzes or puzzles on the topic.
Example:

- A set of six place mats on different biomes of the world (desert, rain forest, deciduous forest, tundra, grassland, and savanna)

3. PHOTO OR MAGAZINE ESSAY:

Use a series of photographs taken with a camera or illustrations collected from popular magazines as a basis for writing an essay on an interesting topic or theme of your choice. Include a brief description of or reference to the photographs or illustrations in one of the paragraphs of your essay.
Examples:

- A group of photographs on architectural styles of special structures in your community
- A collection of magazine illustrations showing different uses or abuse of land in our society

CREATIVE SPRINGBOARDS FOR STUDENT-GENERATED PROJECTS

4. OWNER'S MANUAL OR GUIDEBOOK:
Write a creative owner's manual or guidebook to show others how to take care of an object or how to find their way around a given place.
Examples:
- An owner's manual for taking care of your pet rock or your stamp collection
- A guidebook for taking a kid's tour of the local cemetery or art museum

5. POSTCARDS OR LETTERS:
Design a set of original postcards to show important people, places, or things in a given area, or design a set of unique letters to tell others about important people, places, or things in a given area.
Examples:
- A set of postcards depicting major settings, characters, and events in a novel you have read
- A set of personal letters containing a dialogue on your adventures when traveling back in time or visiting in a foreign country

6. MONUMENTS OR HISTORICAL MARKERS:
Create a series of historical monuments or markers describing and celebrating the contributions of important heroes and events.
Examples:
- A set of plans/illustrations/reasons for a series of living monuments honoring famous women in American history
- A set of historical markers summarizing the major dates and events leading up to the development of the computer

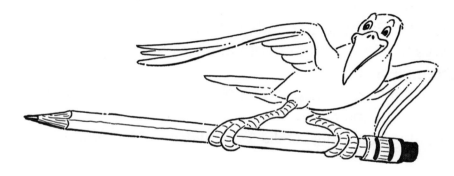

CREATIVE SPRINGBOARDS FOR STUDENT-GENERATED PROJECTS

7. SANDWICH BOARD:
Plan and construct a king-size sandwich
board to wear to inform others about a
topic or subject of interest to you.
Example:
  • A sandwich board summarizing the
    major geometric shapes and formulas
    for their use in the real world

**8. WIND CATCHER OR WIND
SOCK:**
Create and construct an original
wind catcher or wind sock to hang
in the classroom and to share a
series of facts and figures on a
topic you have researched.
Examples:
  • A wind catcher whose body contains
    a picture, diagram, or visual
    illustrating a major concept and
    whose tail streamers contain a series
    of relevant facts or terms
  • A wind sock whose body reflects a detailed model of a gasoline engine or
    an electric circuit

9. FLIP CHART OR BIG BOOK:
Prepare a report that makes use of a flip chart format or that is
recorded in the form of a big book. Both of these options are good
ways to share written information with a large group.
Examples:
  • A flip chart of approximately ten pages outlining the major systems of the
    human body
  • A big book that retells a popular myth or legend

10. ROLLER MOVIE OR SCROLL:

Report your research findings in the form of a roller movie or a scroll. In either case, you will need a roll of plain shelf paper and a pair of dowels or long pencils. A cardboard box with a window opening is also required for the roller movie. Use a storyboard layout to plan your sequence of scenes and information sections for either the movie or scroll.

Examples:

- A roller movie showing the various stages of the growth of plants from your science experiments
- A scroll teaching others about the art and science of making and flying a kite

11. TRADING CARDS:

Design a set of colorful and informative trading cards based on a topic you are studying in class. Model your trading cards after baseball or football cards. Put a graphic or illustration on one side of the card and a set of facts, statistics, terms, or statements on the other side of the card. You may even want to trade or exchange selected cards with your peers in order to study and review concepts for a quiz, discussion, or classroom assignment.

Example:

- A set of trading cards representing famous authors, composers, and artists

12. TRIPTYCH:

You can prepare a three-sided triptych from a cardboard box or by taping three pieces of equal-sized posterboard/construction paper together. A triptych is a freestanding set of three adjacent rectangular panels or sections. The middle section of the triptych typically displays the title and an outline of the major points of the report. The two end panels usually contain written information, charts, graphs, diagrams, and other relevant graphics.

Example:

- A triptych book report of a science fiction novel

13. TOTEM POLE:

Make a king-size totem pole by rolling a large piece of posterboard into a fat cylinder. Then, use a large piece of manila drawing paper or newsprint the same size as the posterboard on which to write your project information. You might want to divide the drawing paper/newsprint into horizontal sections much like those of a real totem pole. Each section may cover a different topic of your report or a different set of sketches/drawings related to your report. After all writing and drawing is completed, paste the drawing paper/newsprint over the posterboard totem pole for display and sharing of information.

Example:

- A history and timeline of a Native American tribe or the California Gold Rush

14. BOOK OF LISTS AND FACTS:

Compile a book of related lists and amazing facts on a topic or theme in any given subject area. These lists may be bound into booklet form, complete with a title page, dedication page, table of contents page, bibliography page, and an all-about-the-author page.

Example:

- A book of lists and facts about the language of mathematics (partial list of contents: geometric formulas, math signs and symbols, measures and weights, number facts, number patterns, number puzzles)

15. WINDOW POSTERS OR GREETING CARDS:

Design a learning poster with lift-up windows or a box of greeting cards with lift-up flaps to teach others about a topic they might find interesting. On the outside of the window, write a question to be answered. Under the lift-up flap and on the window, write the correct response to the question. Add appropriate graphics or diagrams around the edges of the poster or on the covers of the greeting cards to further illustrate the important concepts.

Example:

• Careers in a particular field entitled: "Windows of Opportunity"

16. AUDIO TAPE ESSAYS:

Tape-record an oral report and provide an outline or script for others to follow. Encourage others to take notes while listening to your essay. Design a creative box, envelope, or other container for your audio tape project.

Example:

• An audio essay on tornadoes, hurricanes, and earthquakes

CREATIVE SPRINGBOARDS FOR STUDENT-GENERATED PROJECTS

17. GROUP NEWSPAPER OR MAGAZINE:

Work with a group of peers to produce a newspaper or magazine based on a major theme or interdisciplinary unit that you are studying in class. All content for the newspaper or magazine should reflect topics relevant to that theme and should feature a variety of newspaper writing styles. You may want to assign specific roles such as editor, news reporter, fiction writer, advertising director, cartoonist, etc. Some features that you might want to include in your newspaper or magazine are:

- Name of publication
- Index or table of contents
- Front page or cover of publication
- Editorials and letters to editor
- Classified or display ads
- Comic strips or cartoons
- News or non-fiction articles
- Feature or human interest stories
- Book or movie reviews
- Interviews with important people
- Advice or helpful hints columns
- Informational charts, graphs, or diagrams
- Photographs or illustrations

Examples:
- A newspaper written during the time of the United States Civil War
- A magazine about health and nutrition for kids

18. GROUP POSITION PAPER:

Collaborate with a small group of peers to write a position paper on a controversial topic or issue of importance to you. To begin this task, select a topic and develop an outline of important points, facts, opinions, arguments, and examples that are relevant to the topic and that make sense to each of you. Each person in your group should write a different section of the outline. Once each person has completed his or her section, share and critique these with one another, making certain that there is a logical progression of ideas and that the ideas reflect your positions on the topic or issue.

Example:
- A position paper stating your explanation for the growing number of teenagers who run away, attempt suicide, or abuse substances

66

CREATIVE SPRINGBOARDS FOR STUDENT-GENERATED PROJECTS

19. POETRY NOTEBOOK:

Write poems in a variety of forms to share information about important concepts in any subject area. In addition, collect some poems by well-known poets based on a central theme, copy them in a notebook, and add your own illustrations or reactions to the selections. Choose a concept such as weather, food, shapes, or nature and use any of the following poetry patterns to create original poems that tell others what you have learned. Add poems from your favorite poetry books on the topic as well.

- Haiku
- Tanka
- Diamante
- Free Verse
- Name Poem
- Limerick
- Concrete
- Couplet
- Ballad
- Sonnet

Example:

- Five ways to look at a rainbow (haiku, free verse, concrete, diamante, and couplets)

20. HOW-TO BOOK WITH A HUMOROUS TWIST:

Write your own how-to book by listing the steps for accomplishing a given task or surviving a particular experience. Arrange the steps in the correct order and write each one on a separate page. Be sure to add enough detail to make the directions easy and interesting to read. Try giving your how-to topic a twist by making it humorous and different. For example, why not write the steps for flunking a test, losing a ball game, or getting into trouble at school?

Example:

- How to jinx a lab experiment in science class

CREATIVE SPRINGBOARDS FOR STUDENT-GENERATED PROJECTS

21. HISTORICAL RE-ENACTMENTS:

Create an exciting historical scenario by selecting a special event from history and re-enacting it with a prepared script, live actors, interesting dialogue, and realistic props. Consider the Boston Tea Party, the astronauts' first journey to the moon, the discovery of the polio vaccine, or a jousting tournament during the Middle Ages as possible events to dramatize.
Example:

- A historical re-enactment of a civil rights demonstration in Washington, D.C.

22. ORAL HISTORY OF A MODERN EVENT:

Assume the role of a historian and record the events of an upcoming celebration, incident, milestone, or happening in your school or community. To do this you would have to be physically present at the event with your camera, camcorder, and/or tape recorder to orally and visually record the event. You may also want to conduct interviews with participants and patrons to identify their perceptions of the event. Also consider recording rich descriptions of the people, places, and things that you observe.
Example:

- An oral history of the dedication of the new media center at school

23. SHOEBOX MINI-PARADE:

Parade possibilities exist in any subject area: floats representing varied countries around the world, floats representing different biomes, floats representing favorite novels, or floats representing milestones in mathematics are all possibilities. Make your parade of floats out of shoeboxes and decorate them with cut-outs, recycled odds and ends (wooden spools, ribbon, cloth, etc.), and clay figures. Toy trucks can move the parade down the street. Create a script stating the purpose, history, and other important details about each of the floats.
Example:

- Parade of floats representing characters and events from mythology

USING PROMPTS AS SPRINGBOARDS FOR READING, WRITING, COMPUTING, AND THINKING ACTIVITIES

DIRECTIONS:

A "prompt" is a brief description of a learning activity that can be used as a springboard for practicing reading, writing, computing, and thinking activities. Choose one or more of the following prompts to use to complete a product for assessment purposes.

MATH PROMPT

Use the number sentence (equation) below to complete these exercises:

    a. Write a word problem to go with the equation.

    b. Draw a picture to go with the equation.

    c. Make up additional equations of your own and tell about them in creative ways such as through pictures, stories, word problems, or rhymes. Can you create equations that use fractions, decimals, and percentages?

EQUATION: 1/10 of 200 = 20

LANGUAGE ARTS PROMPT

Locate an interesting picture in a magazine. Cut it out and paste it on a piece of drawing paper. Use the picture to complete the writing exercises below:

(1) Write one declarative, one interrogative, one imperative, and one exclamatory sentence about the picture.

(2) Write one fact and one opinion statement about the picture.

(3) Write one compound and one complex sentence about the picture.

(4) Write a sentence that contains a direct or indirect quotation about the picture.

(5) Write a title for the picture.

SOCIAL STUDIES PROMPT

Who invented ice cream? How did velcro get its funny name? Why was the atomic bomb created? Inventors and their inventions have had a significant impact on our world. Select an invention that you feel best fits each category below. For each invention, tell who, what, when, where, why, and how:

(1) An invention that revolutionized industry

(2) An invention that saved lives

(3) An invention from nature

(4) An invention by accident

(5) A failed invention that eventually succeeded

SCIENCE PROMPT

Go on an Ecology Walk around your school. The purpose of your walk is to look for examples of pollution and environmental waste present in such places as the cafeteria, media center, restroom, playground, custodial office, and classrooms. Record all of the problems you see. When you return to the classroom, write a summary of your findings and offer some possible suggestions for improving or solving the problems listed. Create a poster, chart, graph, or other display to assist you with sharing your ideas. Be convincing and try to persuade others to take action.

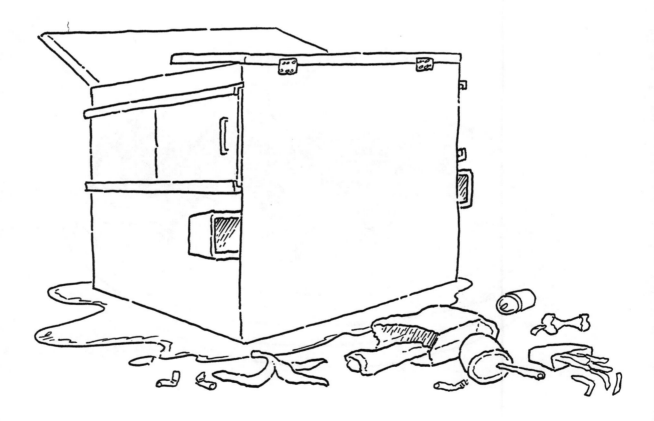

USING A THEMATIC MINI-UNIT WITH
A LANGUAGE ARTS FOCUS
TO DEVELOP A PRODUCT EXHIBIT

DIRECTIONS:

*B*ook Look is a thematic mini-unit that has been developed to help you extend and make meaningful use of basic language arts and critical thinking skills and develop a deeper appreciation of literature.

After completing all of the activities according to the directions, select one piece of work to use as your product exhibit.

Write a detailed paragraph in the space below explaining the particular piece of work you selected as your product exhibit. Include a brief description of the piece of work that would have been your last choice for developing a product. Be sure to state the reasons you feel as you do about both pieces of work.

_____

_____

_____

_____

_____

_____

_____

_____

_____

_____

_____

_____

_____

_____

_____

Name _____ Date _____

BOOK LOOK

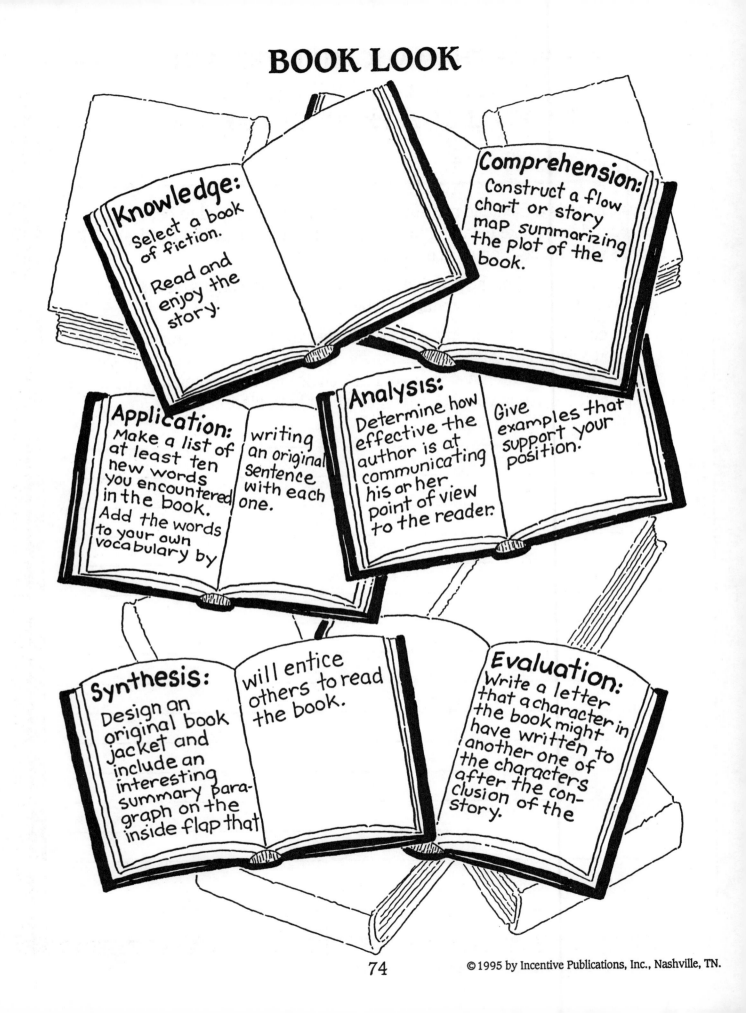

Knowledge:
Select a book of fiction.

Read and enjoy the story.

Comprehension:
Construct a flow chart or story map summarizing the plot of the book.

Application:
Make a list of at least ten new words you encountered in the book. Add the words to your own vocabulary by writing an original sentence with each one.

Analysis:
Determine how effective the author is at communicating his or her point of view to the reader. Give examples that support your position.

Synthesis:
Design an original book jacket and include an interesting summary paragraph on the inside flap that will entice others to read the book.

Evaluation:
Write a letter that a character in the book might have written to another one of the characters after the conclusion of the story.

DIRECTIONS:

You are often asked to prepare a report for some teacher or class, and it is important that you try to be creative in the way you present information from your research. The following ten report formats are suggestions for you to try. They would make excellent artifacts for your portfolio, or they could be used as springboards for preparing a report to be shared verbally with your classmates.

FOUR-POINT SQUARE

You will need a 9-inch square of heavy construction paper or drawing paper. Fold the paper into fourths and then open it up again. Fold each corner of the square so that it touches the center. On the outside of each flap, write: WHO, WHAT, WHERE/WHEN, and WHY. Choose a person to study for your report. Write the title of your report and your name as author in the center of the opened square. Write a brief response on the underside of each flap describing the WHO, WHAT, WHERE/WHEN, and WHY information you have learned.

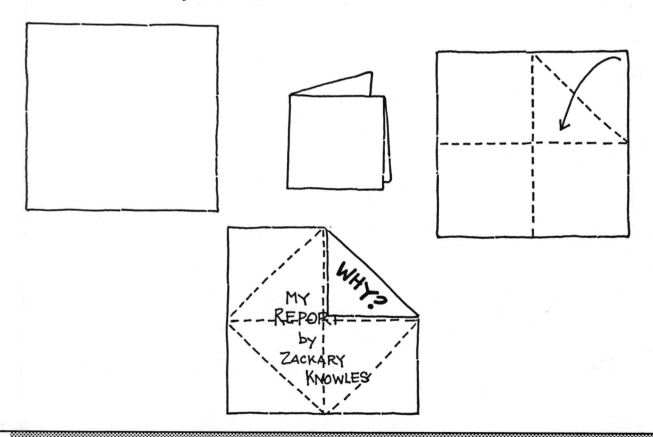

FLIP AND TELL

Decide on the number of pages you want your Stagger Flip Report to contain. On each page use a ruler to mark off equal segments of approximately one inch, so that each page is one inch shorter than the one underneath it. For example, the back page should be a full-size piece of paper. The page directly on top of the back page should be cut one inch shorter in length. Repeat this process for each page. The first page should be the smallest in size. Staple the pages together at the top, from smallest to largest, to produce a staggered effect. Select a topic for your report and write a set of questions to research about the topic. The first page of your book (the shortest page) will be the cover of your report, containing the title and your name as author.

Write a question along the bottom edge of each page. Each question should appear in the staggered margins in order to be visible when the book is closed. Use the rest of the page to answer the question. Predict the length of your responses so that the longer pages will contain the questions requiring the longest answers.

MOVIE MAGIC

Select a topic and write a short report on it, using pictures with short statements, or record an audio tape commentary to go with each segment. When the illustrations and statements are completed, transfer them onto "frames" which have been marked off on a long strip of oak tag or posterboard. Construct a slide projector using a shoe box turned upside-down. Cut a peephole at one end of the box. At the opposite end of the box, cut narrow slits through which to slide the storyboard. Cut another larger slit in the top of the projector through which to allow light to shine.

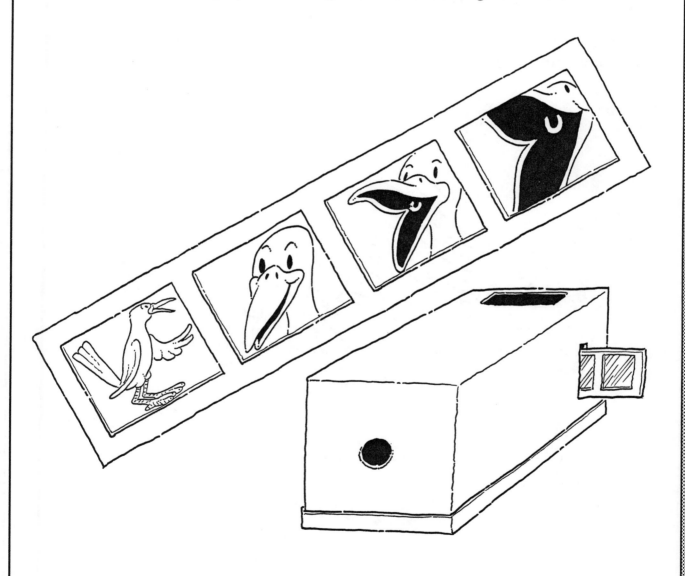

SHAPE-UP

Choose a topic and research to find out information on the topic. Then select several symbols that are representative of your topic. For example, if you are writing an Americana report you might choose the Liberty Bell, an eagle, a flag, the Capitol building, and the Washington Monument as symbols. Draw a large outline of each symbol on individual file folders and cut them out.

Make a cardboard tripod with slits (as used with paper dolls) for each symbol so that they become freestanding. Write and record your paragraphs on lined paper and glue these to the appropriate cut-out symbols. Number the paragraphs in the correct sequence and stand them up for reading and display.

FOLD-OVER, FOLD-OUT

Select a topic to report on and write a series of comprehensive paragraphs on the topic. Make up a thought-provoking question about each paragraph. Use 5" x 8" unlined file cards, or cut oak tag into 5" x 8" rectangles. Fasten the ends of the cards together using transparent tape and fold the cards back and forth to form an accordion book. Create an interesting cover for your book and include a short paragraph about yourself. Begin your report on the second card of the book. Write a corresponding question for the reader to answer based on information he or she has just read. Continue in this manner until all sections of your accordion book have been completed and all paragraphs of your report have been addressed.

BOOK IN A POCKET

Select a topic for your report and write ten unusual or interesting questions. Use 8½" x 11" pieces of oak tag or heavy manila drawing paper to make your pocket booklet, allowing one sheet for each question. Decorate a piece of oak tag for your front and back covers and use staples, rings, or brass fasteners to attach the pages together. At the bottom of each page, glue an empty envelope with the flap side up to the bottom of the page. In the space above the envelope, write one of the questions in big letters and illustrate it with clues in some way. Write the answer to the question in significant detail on a small 3" x 5" file card, and slip it into the envelope. People who read your report will first look at the question, try to answer it, and then take out the card to check their answers against the "expert" on the subject. "Everything You Wanted To Know About _____ But Were Afraid To Ask!" is a suggested title for your book.

PUZZLE TO SOLVE

Choose a topic to research and write your information on a piece of oak tag or posterboard. Use a size that is appropriate for the quantity of information you wish to share. After recording your report on the oak tag or posterboard, turn it over and randomly draw a puzzle pattern of up to six to eight pieces using a pencil. Cut apart the pieces and store them in a resealable bag. Exchange your puzzle report with your classmates to discuss and solve.

WORK IN PROGRESS

Choose a topic to research. Before beginning your investigation, divide a piece of legal size paper (8½" x 14") into three equal columns. Label the first column WHAT I KNOW; label the second column WHAT I WANT TO KNOW; and label the third column WHAT I LEARNED. Fill in the information for the first and second columns. As you conduct your research, you can complete the third column.

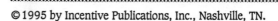

FABULOUS FACT CARDS

Work with a small group of peers to research a topic that appeals to each of you. Divide the topic into subtopics. Assign each person a different subtopic to research and record facts about. Prepare a set of blank fact cards using unlined 5" x 8" file cards for this purpose. On one side of each fact card, write the following words at the top: A CHART (GRAPH, DIAGRAM, or MAP) ABOUT MY FABULOUS FACT. Write these words at the bottom: Prepared By _____

On the other side of each fact card, write the following words at the top: MY FABULOUS FACT READS and record the information about the facts that you have studied. It is important that you use a separate fact card for each fact. When all members of your group have completed their assigned research and fact cards, exchange them with one another. Together, prepare an outline of the combined information gathered from this collaborative effort.

Adapted from an idea by: Christine Boardman Moen, *Better Than Book Reports*. Scholastic: New York, New York, 1992.

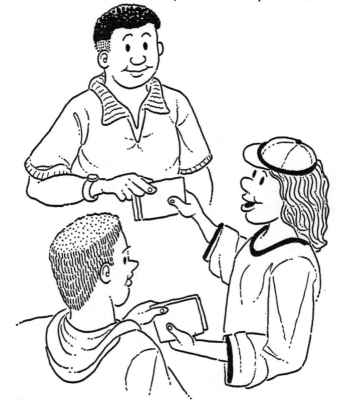

COMIC STRIP REPORT

Place a piece of 12" x 18" white drawing paper in front of you so that it is 18 inches wide and 12 inches high. Fold the paper in half from the bottom up. Open the paper and fold it in half the other way. Fold once more, making a total of eight sections. Trace the creases dividing the sections with a heavy black marker. Choose a topic for your comic strip report. In the top left section, write your report title and personal information. Create a cartoon character related to your topic. In each of the remaining seven sections, have your character share facts about your topic. Illustrate your comic strip.

RUBRIC FOR EVALUATING MY PROJECT

DIRECTIONS:

Using this rubric, evaluate the different elements of your project with your teacher.

STUDENT NAME _____ TEACHER NAME _____

DATE OF EVALUATION _____ PROJECT TOPIC _____

RATE EACH OF THE ELEMENTS OF YOUR PROJECT USING THIS ANALYTIC
RATING SCALE: 3 = Excellent   2 = Good   1 = Fair   0 = No Evidence

ELEMENTS OF PROJECT TO BE EVALUATED:

	STUDENT	TEACHER
1. Choice of topic		
2. Guiding questions or objectives		
3. Quality of research		
4. Organization		
5. Knowledge of topic		
6. Imagination or creativity		
7. Use of visuals		
8. Degree of effort		

WHAT DO YOU THINK WAS THE BEST THING ABOUT THIS PROJECT?

Student _____

Teacher _____

WHAT DO YOU THINK COULD BE IMPROVED MOST ON THIS PROJECT?

Student _____

Teacher _____

HOW DOES THIS PROJECT COMPARE WITH OTHERS YOU HAVE COMPLETED
IN PAST CLASSES OR YEARS?

_____

_____

Making
PERFORMANCES
Meaningful
and
Manageable

A BIRD'S EYE VIEW OF STUDENT PERFORMANCES

WHAT IS PERFORMANCE ASSESSMENT?

Performance assessment is an active evaluation process that involves presenting students with a task, project, or investigation, and then observing, interviewing, and looking at their productions to assess what they actually know and can do. Observation of a student's actual performance is already common practice in many areas. In sports, for example, individuals and teams have tryouts and games. In music and drama, individuals perform on an instrument or act on stage before a director in order to gain a place in a musical group or theatrical troupe.

A BIRD'S EYE VIEW OF STUDENT PERFORMANCES

WHY IS PERFORMANCE ASSESSMENT A VALUABLE EVALUATION TOOL?

Performance assessment measures are flexible because they can be used with both individuals and groups. They allow the teacher to examine the learning process as well as the end result. Finally, through observations and interviews, performance assessments can document a wide variety of learning experiences and accomplishments that cannot be revealed by traditional paper-and-pencil tests.

WHAT ARE SOME ADVANTAGES OF PERFORMANCE ASSESSMENT FOR THE STUDENT?

Because performances are applications of learning, they provide students with opportunities to display many aspects of their skills and knowledge, not just speed and accuracy. In addition, students generally find performance assessment tasks to be more relevant, creative, and challenging than other types of tests. Furthermore, performance assessment is highly motivating to students because it involves choice and empowers the learner to have some control over the assessment process.

A BIRD'S EYE VIEW OF STUDENT PERFORMANCES

WHAT ARE SOME TYPES OF PERFORMANCE ASSESSMENTS?

Performing a science experiment, acting in a play, staging a debate, giving an oral book report, conducting active research, creating a newspaper, and giving a speech are all types of performance assessment. Other types of performance assessment include putting on displays or exhibits and planning fairs, festivals, or carnivals.

HOW SHOULD PERFORMANCE ASSESSMENTS BE EVALUATED?

Performance tasks should be evaluated by the teacher or by a panel of peers and/or outside observers. Whether the performance assessment focuses on a group of students or on an individual, the assessment can take many forms, such as:

(1) presenting students with a problem and listening to their responses;

(2) observing what students do and say during a learning task;

(3) interviewing students during or after an investigation; and/or

(4) collecting evidence of student achievement through their product, exhibit, or project results.

INTRODUCING AND SHARING PERFORMANCE ASSESSMENT WITH YOUR FAMILY

DIRECTIONS: (Step One)

You will be involved in a series of performances in this class that will make up a significant portion of your grade for this marking period. When members of your family and/or other important adults in your life know and understand how performance assessment works, the performances themselves become more meaningful for them and for you. By informing and involving them in the entire performance experience, they will understand the assessment criteria to be used and will be better able to share in your excitement related to the performance. They will also be more able to help you determine your own progress and plan realistically for future performances. Performance projects can actually become meaningful and effective channels for sharing personal experiences and feelings with your family. To accomplish this, make sure everyone understands how and why you chose the particular type of performance as well as the criteria for evaluation. Begin by carefully reading through the "Bird's Eye View" on pages 87-89 and discussing it with your teachers and classmates to be sure you have a thorough understanding of what performances are all about. Now you are ready to share and explain the "Bird's Eye View" of performance assessment to your parents and/or other important adults in your life.

90

INTRODUCING AND SHARING PERFORMANCE ASSESSMENT WITH YOUR FAMILY

DIRECTIONS: (Step Two)

When your performance presentation is complete, you will be sharing it with your parents and/or other important adults in your life. It is important that they understand what you did to prepare for the performance from start to finish, how the performance was evaluated, and how you feel about the experience. It is equally important for all of you to engage in an open and non-threatening discussion of your growth from the performance and how using presentation assessment compares to more traditional forms of evaluation. In instances where the presentation was created as a part of or as a result of a group effort, you will need to identify the other group members, explain your contribution to the project, and discuss the game plan and goals behind the activity. When explaining your performance, include specific details as to the criteria used by your teachers to give input in the developmental stages and in the final assessment of the completed performance. Your family's feedback and suggestions can be extremely helpful in planning and organizing your next performance. For this reason, ask your family members to complete the Parent Performance Assessment Feedback Form (page 92) and return it to your teacher as promptly as possible.

PARENT PERFORMANCE ASSESSMENT FEEDBACK FORM

MY CHILD'S NAME _____ DATE_____

FAMILY MEMBERS PRESENT FOR PERFORMANCE EXPLANATION

_____

_____

1. What was your initial reaction to the idea of performance assessment in our class?

   _____

2. In your opinion, what are the advantages and disadvantages of performance assessment for your child?

   _____

3. List some performance experiences which your child has had at home or in the community.

   _____

   _____

4. Check the type of performances that you think would be most effective for your child to try:

   ____ Play or Skit   ____ Exhibit or Display
   ____ Demonstration   ____ Discussion
   ____ Mock Trial   ____ Mock Television/Radio Show
   ____ Fair or Carnival   ____ Experiment
   ____ Case Study or Role-play   ____ Debate or Panel
   ____ Speech or Oral Presentation ____ Other (Please Specify)

   _____

5. How do you think performance assessment compares to more traditional methods (tests, etc.) of measuring your child's progress?

   _____

COMMENTS:

Signed_____

TEACHER'S PERFORMANCE PLANNING GUIDELINES

DIRECTIONS:

Review these guidelines for designing a performance task for your subject area and group of students.

EIGHT QUESTIONS TO ANSWER
WHEN EXPLORING A PERFORMANCE TASK:

1. Does the performance task fit the essential objectives of your discipline by focusing on a "big idea"?

2. Does the performance task include process skills appropriate for the discipline so that it will be valued by students?

3. Does the performance task raise other questions and lead to other problems or possibilities?

4. Does the performance task include thought-provoking ideas and issues?

5. Does the performance task require the student to make decisions and interact with other students in a search for meaning and understanding?

6. Does the performance task meet the time and energy requirements of the student so that it is feasible and developmentally appropriate?

7. Does the performance task cater to a variety of learning styles?

8. Does the performance task have more than one right answer or approach for finding a right answer?

GUIDELINES FOR PLANNING A STUDENT PERFORMANCE

DIRECTIONS:

When your teacher asks you to prepare and deliver a student performance to show what you know and what you can do in a given subject area or on a given topic, it is important that you follow a set of guidelines for making the performance a success. Use these guidelines in helping you plan your next performance task.

1. Be able to relate your performance to specific skills, concepts, and objectives required of you for a specific content area.

2. Be able to clearly explain the purpose and expected outcome of your performance to your teacher and peers.

3. Be able to view or discuss examples of high-quality performances done by students in other classes.

4. Be able to identify a list of criteria that would constitute a high-quality performance.

5. Be able to consider several choices when selecting the final topic for your performance.

6. Be able to plan, monitor, and evaluate your progress while working on your performance.

7. Be able to practice and give the performance for the teacher, class, and/or an outside audience.

8. Be able to conduct a self-evaluation of your performance using the criteria listed in number four above.

9. Be able to discuss feedback on your performance with teachers, peers, or members of an outside audience.

10. Be able to set new goals for your next performance based on the feedback you received from yourself and others.

11. Be able to use the critiques of the performance as an artifact in your portfolio.

SAMPLE INDEPENDENT STUDY CONTRACT
FOR A PERFORMANCE OR PROJECT

DIRECTIONS:

Sometimes it is helpful to design a contract before starting a major project or performance assessment task. This contract will help you plan your work, and it will let your teacher know what is expected from both you and him or her during the project/performance development process.

Name _____ Grade/Subject _____

Beginning date of project/performance work_____

Planned completion/delivery date of project/performance_____

Statement of problems to be researched/studied_____

_____

_____

Goals/objectives to be accomplished through project/performance

_____

_____

Format of project/performance_____

Intended audience for project/performance _____

Proposed steps for completing my project/performance

  1. Information/data/resources I will use _____

    _____

  2. Technical help I will need from others _____

    _____

  3. Special equipment/materials I will require _____

    _____

Signature of student_____

Signature of teacher _____

Date _____ Place_____

AN OUTLINE FOR PLANNING A DISPLAY OR EXHIBITION

DIRECTIONS:

In planning a display or exhibit, it is sometimes wise to develop a comprehensive outline for, or vision of, the finished product. Once your plan is complete, you can use it to "work backwards" when deciding on the details for content, skills, materials, and time lines.

1. What general learner outcomes do you wish to accomplish through your display or exhibit?

   _____

   _____

   _____

2. What will the final display or exhibit look like? Draw a sketch on another piece of paper.

   _____

   _____

   _____

3. What specific subject area facts, principles, concepts, or terms do you wish to teach or feature in your display or exhibit?

   _____

   _____

   _____

4. What specific skills do you wish to demonstrate or focus on in your display or exhibit?

   _____

   _____

   _____

Name _____ Date _____

PLANNING A PEOPLE SEARCH MINI-PERFORMANCE WITH A NEW TWIST

DIRECTIONS:

Find someone in the group who can provide an accurate answer for each of the items listed here and have them sign their names in the appropriate spaces. Note that only one person in the group can sign for one item on your paper. Make certain the person knows the answer to the item before signing by having him or her give you a sample response in advance.

At the conclusion of this simple performance task, the teacher will conduct a group discussion and call on students to give individual responses for any item they acknowledge on the People Search Forms. Incorrect responses will be modified at this time.

PEOPLE SEARCH FORM

Based on our recent chemistry unit,
my signature shows you that I . . .

1. . . . can define matter. _____

2. . . . can identify the different states of matter. _____

3. . . . can give three examples of chemical reactions. _____

4. . . . can explain physical and chemical properties. _____

5. . . . can describe a physical change. _____

6. . . . can describe a chemical change. _____

7. . . . can compare acids and bases. _____

8. . . . can give examples of metals and non-metals. _____

9. . . . can list at least ten different elements. _____

10. . . . can define a compound. _____

11. . . . can tell you what an atom is. _____

12. . . . can name the three particles of an atom. _____

Name _____ Date _____

SHARING A CULTURAL ARTIFACT KIT
WITH YOUR PEERS

DIRECTIONS:

Select a country that is of particular interest to you. Prepare an artifact kit of approximately ten items representative of that country's geography, history, climate, economy, customs, languages, religions, tourist attractions, people, art, and music. Use personal drawings, real or imitation objects, descriptions, posters, postcards, and photographs for this purpose.

Create an information file card about each artifact and attach it to the appropriate item. Use these cards to prepare and deliver a short presentation of approximately ten minutes in length for your class. Use the outline below in planning your "Cultural Artifact Kit." Write your responses on a separate piece of paper. Be sure to include a simple quiz in your kit that could be used to determine what the audience learned from your presentation. The rubric below should be used by the members of the audience to evaluate your performance.

QUESTION OUTLINE TO COMPLETE:

1. What country did you select ? Why did you make this choice?
2. What are some interesting facts about the country's geography, history, climate, economy, customs, languages, religions, tourist attractions, people, art, and music?
3. What are some artifacts that you were able to locate or create for your kit and presentation?
4. What ideas do you have for opening and closing remarks of your presentation?
5. What type of container or packaging will you use and/or decorate for your kit?

RUBRIC FOR CULTURAL KIT PRESENTATION:
3 = Great   2 = Good   1 = Fair   0 = No Evidence

_____ 1. Presenter was prepared and organized.

_____ 2. Presenter had effective opening and closing statements.

_____ 3. Presenter used ten artifacts in the delivery of the information.

_____ 4. Presenter spoke clearly and slowly for understanding.

_____ 5. Presenter showed enthusiasm for his or her country.

_____ 6. Presenter was creative in his or her choice of ideas and artifacts.

_____ 7. Presenter adhered to proper time limit for presentation.

_____ 8. Presenter covered all of the required cultural dimensions in some way.

_____ 9. Presenter made the presentation interesting and informative.

_____ 10. Presenter included a quiz in the kit.

TOTAL POSSIBLE POINTS = 30

DIRECTING AND PERFORMING A CHORAL SPEAKING ACTIVITY

DIRECTIONS:

Choral reading is a small or large group recitation of poetry. It provides students with opportunities to improve their diction, voice projection, ability to follow directions, and appreciation of literature. Pretend that you are going to lead a group of peers in a choral reading activity. To do this, you are to follow the steps listed below for preparing yourself and others for the task. Remember that practice makes perfect, so get busy and have fun!

Step One: Select a short poem from a favorite poet such as Eve Merriam or Shel Silverstein. Practice reading it aloud with expression, pronouncing the words clearly (diction) and speaking with a firm voice (projection).

Step Two: Choose five or six students to perform the choral reading, with you as their leader. Use your hands and facial expressions to help the students begin and end the poem at the same time, much like the conductor of an orchestra would.

Step Three: Recite the entire poem, line by line, for the group of students using your best expression. Then, recite the poem again one line at a time. You should pause after each line so that the group is able to repeat it, imitating your rhythm, voice inflection, pronunciation, and timing. Repeat this process several times. Try reciting two or three lines at a time and having the others follow your speaking patterns.

Step Four: Select additional poems to use for this choral reading exercise, adding other techniques to the choral reading such as assigning different parts to groups of kids or including a few solo parts.

Step Five: Plan a simple performance of choral readings for another class or group of parents.

Step Six: To help you get started, write down the titles and authors of several poems that you could use for this purpose.

TITLE OF POEM:	**AUTHOR:**
_____	_____
_____	_____
_____	_____
_____	_____

Name _____ Date _____

PERFORMING A CHALK TALK REPORT

DIRECTIONS:

Chalk Talks enable you to give oral reports on assigned topics or themes in a social studies, science, math, or language arts setting. Make a list of eight to ten facts or pieces of information that are important and relevant to the subject of study. Use these facts to create a simple drawing or a series of illustrations on the chalkboard (or the overhead projector) to highlight those same major concepts being described. Each fact stated orally should be accompanied by corresponding lines or objects in the picture so that a completed scene, item, or diagram is visible at the conclusion of the Chalk Talk.

One way to prepare for a Chalk Talk performance is to make a storyboard of eight to ten blank comic strip frames. In each frame, record one fact and a simple set of corresponding lines or drawings. Then, related facts and lines are added in a progressive sequence until both the report and the illustration are complete.

Write down some possible topics and related figures or scenes that you would consider for this activity in the spaces below.

POSSIBLE TOPICS:	POSSIBLE FIGURES/SETTINGS:
_____	_____
_____	_____
_____	_____
_____	_____
_____	_____
_____	_____
_____	_____
_____	_____
_____	_____

Name_____ Date _____

PERFORMING A MONOLOGUE

DIRECTIONS:

A monologue is a long speech made by a single person. It can also mean a humorous story or series of jokes told by a single person. Puns, satire, jokes, slang, illogical conclusions, ridiculous situations, and silly comparisons are some of the techniques used to make these one-person speeches funny. People like Bob Hope, Johnny Carson, and Jay Leno are famous for their opening monologues on nighttime television.

Select one of these subjects listed below for writing your own funny monologue. Practice presenting your monologue in front of a mirror and then perform it for members of your class. Write down four or five criteria on which you want people to judge you while performing your monologue.

SUBJECTS TO CONSIDER:

1. A Martian Watching His First Football Game Or Wrestling Match
2. A Grandmother Trying To Learn To Dance To A Rock-And-Roll Band
3. A Door-To-Door Salesman Trying To Sell Something That Nobody Wants
4. A Real Estate Salesman Trying To Sell A Haunted House
5. A Weather Forecaster Trying To Accurately Predict Your State's Weather
6. A Fashion Designer Trying To Sell A Ridiculous New Style
7. A Beautician Introducing A New Hair Style For Boys And Girls
8. An Interview With A Dumb But Popular Movie Star
9. A Newspaper Reporter Giving An Account Of The First UFO Landing In The United States
10. What It's Like To Be An Old Shoe

CRITERIA TO BE USED IN JUDGING MY MONOLOGUE PERFORMANCE:

1. _____
2. _____
3. _____
4. _____
5. _____

Name _____ Date _____

GIVING AN ORAL PERFORMANCE BASED ON QUOTATIONS FROM MY FAVORITE BOOK OR AUTHOR

DIRECTIONS:

Choose a favorite character from a book, or author of a novel, that you either are currently reading or have read in the recent past. Make a list of your favorite passages from the book or quotations from the author. Use these quotations or passages as springboards for writing your own reaction/interpretation/application of each idea presented. Be prepared to share your thoughts with the class in an oral presentation.

To give you practice with this assignment, try writing a response of at least one paragraph for each of these well-known sayings from the writing of Mark Twain. Compose your paragraphs on a separate piece of paper and practice reciting your words aloud in front of a mirror. Try to use your paragraph as notes only. Don't read your paragraph word-for-word if you can help it!

QUOTATION ONE "Everyone is a moon and has a dark side which he never shows to anybody."

QUOTATION TWO "Man will do many things to get himself loved; he will do all things to get himself envied."

QUOTATION THREE "The man with a new idea is a crank until the idea succeeds."

Name _____ Date _____

PERFORMING AS A FAMILY HISTORIAN

DIRECTIONS:

You will be assuming the role of a historian who is recording the history of you and other members of your family. A historian is a student of past history and an observer and interpreter of current historical events.

Pretend that you are a historian trying to reconstruct the past life of selected family members and past events as well as trying to record events of the present for future reference. Complete each of the activities outlined below in your performance as a historian.

Activity One: Compile a scrapbook that contains artifacts representative of your family and its current lifestyle. Include drawings, clippings, photographs, menus, essays, articles, messages, sales receipts, lists, mail samples, recipes, and anything else you can think of. Bring your scrapbook to class and exchange it with a peer. Try to write a "family biography" of the other person's life at home using only the artifacts in the scrapbook.

Activity Two: Pretend that you are an archaeologist and your home is an archeological site. Collect at least ten family possessions of special interest to you and use these to reconstruct your family's history.

Activity Three: Contact a relative, such as a grandparent or an aunt or uncle, and ask that person to loan you the oldest object in his or her home. Interview your relative to find out the age of the object, the origin of the object, the value of the object, the uses of the object, and the importance of the object. Summarize your findings in a descriptive essay.

Activity Four: Ask your parents or grandparents for copies of old family photographs taken long before you were born. Instruct this person(s) not to tell you anything about the subjects in the photographs until you have examined them in detail. Write down your theories about the photographs and have the family member verify your ideas or correct any false impressions that you had.

PERFORMING YOUR ROLE AS A
CONSUMER ANALYST FOR KIDS

DIRECTIONS:

You are a child advocate who writes product reviews for items that are popular with young consumers. You have been asked to recommend the best buy or value in candy bars for an article to be published in a kid's magazine. As an analyst, you are to answer the following questions to help you make your recommendations and write your review.

1. Why do kids like candy bars?

   _____

   _____

2. Examine five different brands of candy bars that are approximately the same size. Compare weight, ingredients, price, calories, nutrients, and type of packaging/wrappers. List the information in chart form on a separate piece of paper.

3. Does one brand of candy bar have something special or different to offer that the others do not have? Explain.

   _____

   _____

   _____

4. Rank each of the candy bars from your first choice to your last choice in terms of which ones you would buy or recommend that others buy. Give reasons for your choices.

   _____

   _____

   _____

   _____

   _____

NOW . . . organize a "taste test" for these candy bars to determine which candy bar has the best flavor. Outline your plan on a separate piece of paper.

Name _____ Date _____

PLANNING A PERSONIFICATION PERFORMANCE

DIRECTIONS:

Personification is a concept often associated with poetry, although it can be used in a variety of other contexts and subject areas as well. Personification involves the act of giving human-like qualities to inanimate objects or the act of assigning human-like attributes to non-human creatures. Use the space provided on page 106 to write an imaginary story on one of the following topics. Assume the role and identity of the object itself. In writing your story, tell such things as how you feel, what you think, what you do, how you behave, where you go, why you believe what you do, and with whom you associate.

SCIENCE:
1. My Life as a Pine Cone in the Black Forest
2. My Life as a Sedimentary Rock in the Grand Canyon
3. My Life as a Mountain Peak in the Rockies
4. My Life as a Pumpkin Seed in a North Dakota Pumpkin Patch
5. My Life as a Kangaroo in Australia
6. My Life as a Tooth in a Shark

SOCIAL STUDIES:
1. My Life as a Cannon in the Revolutionary War
2. My Life as a Painting in the Vatican
3. My Life as a Kimono in a Japanese Tea House
4. My Life as a Jet in a Metropolitan Airport
5. My Life as a Globe in a Travel Agency
6. My Life as a New Dollar Bill in the U.S. Treasury Department

MATHEMATICS:
1. My Life as a Floppy Disk in a Computer
2. My Life as a Cash Register in a Supermarket
3. My Life as a Protractor in a Geometry Class
4. My Life as a Meter Stick in a Textile Mill
5. My Life as a Calculator in an Accountant's Office
6. My Life as a Stop Watch in the Olympics

LANGUAGE ARTS:
1. My Life as a Dictionary in a Publishing House
2. My Life as a Picture Book in a Public Library
3. My Life as a Red Pencil in an English Classroom
4. My Life as a Best Seller in a Bookstore
5. My Life as a Bookmark in a Lost Novel
6. My Life as a Blank Book in a Teenager's Room

PERSONIFICATION PERFORMANCE

Write your story in the "first person" and be ready to read it aloud to the rest of the class using your best diction, expression, and voice projection.

"I _____

_____

_____

_____

_____

_____

_____

_____

_____

_____

_____

_____

_____

_____

_____

_____

_____

_____

_____

_____

_____

_____

_____

Name _____ Date _____

Title _____

PERFORMING SCIENCE ON STAGE

DIRECTIONS:

The use of drama in a science classroom can be a great learning experience for students who learn best from hands-on experiences. The following ideas are springboards for creative dramatics; they provide opportunities for students to translate science concepts into live productions. Try it, you'll like it!

SPRINGBOARD ONE: Draw a diagram of an important food chain you have researched for science class. Consider a food chain such as the sun-grass-mouse-snake-owl-fungus decomposition scenario. Create a ballet of this series of events set to a piece of classical music such as Vivaldi's Four Seasons. Mimic the actions of each of the food chain elements with your body to create elegant movements much like those executed by a ballerina.

SPRINGBOARD TWO: Create a series of pantomimes or pageantry scenes that present important science concepts such as photosynthesis, pollination, metamorphosis, erosion, ecosystems, carbon cycle, recycling, extinction, or weather formations. Stage your productions and have the audience try to guess the ideas you are trying to portray. Write a series of science terms and their corresponding definitions to consider using in this exercise.

SPRINGBOARD THREE: Stage a parade of living floats that highlight several science concepts ranging from "life cycle of the butterfly" to "formation of star patterns in the night sky." Sketch a rough outline or copy of a float with a science theme that appeals to you. Then try to make it come alive!

PLANNING AND TEACHING A VIDEO LESSON

DIRECTIONS:

Video tapes can be excellent teaching tools for the classroom. There are many video tape selections on a wide variety of subject areas available through your school media center or through a video rental store. Develop a lesson plan for using one of these video tapes to teach the other students in the class something about a topic of interest to you. In planning your presentation, try to follow the steps listed below.

1. Preview the video several times. Take notes on the important concepts discussed in the video. If it is a long video, you may want to show only excerpts of the program, concentrating on the most relevant points.

2. Make a list of the most important ideas described in the video and think of instructional activities that you might have students do to reinforce these ideas.

3. Plan a series of active learning experiences to use with the students before, during, and after the viewing. Make these activities relevant, interactive, and interesting. Consider using a short writing task, a small group discussion, a set of open-ended questions, a quiz, a puzzle, or a think/pair/share activity.

4. Provide a focus for viewing each segment of the video so that the students know in advance what to look for or what to take notes on.

5. Pause every so often to check students' understanding of the video. Try asking students to make predictions, give summaries, draw conclusions, or review key ideas as part of this process.

6. Try turning off the sound or the picture at strategic times during the viewing of the video to give students a chance to practice their listening or observation skills.

PERFORMING AS A MOVIE, BOOK, TELEVISION, OR RESTAURANT CRITIC

DIRECTIONS:

Many people make their living critiquing the products and services of others. To help you get started learning more about these careers, research the meaning of such terms as "review," "critique," "analyze," "summarize," "evaluate," "opinions," and "documentation." Relate each of these words to the role of an art critic, a food critic, or a drama critic.

Next, locate a variety of reviews from your local newspaper. Look for critiques of plays, restaurants, books, movies, and television shows. Determine the elements of a good review, such as an opening lead, a synopsis, an appraisal of an individual/group performance, and a rating of some type.

Finally, prepare a review of your own that critiques either a new book for teenage readers, a restaurant that is popular with young customers, a movie that has been released for general viewing, or a television show that has high ratings with adolescents. Be prepared to share your review in an oral presentation. Outline the criteria you will use in this critique after completing the following questions.

1. What will you critique? Will it be a book, restaurant, movie, or television show? What is its name or title, and why did you choose this particular item or situation?

2. What elements will you examine in your review? Are you concerned with characters, plot, conflict, service, size/time, performance, audience reaction, novelty, creativity, interest level, relevance, etc.?

3. How will you collect your data for the review, and how will you organize the information you collected?

4. On a scale of one to four, how many stars would you give this book, restaurant, movie, or television show, and why?

PLANNING AN ECOLOGY FESTIVAL
FOR YOUR CLASS

DIRECTIONS:

You will be working with a group of peers to plan an Ecology Festival for members of your class. Although this event can be arranged to celebrate Earth Day, April 22, it can take place any time of year. Below are some suggestions for you to consider in planning the festival. You will also want to add others of your own.

1. **INVITATIONS:** Decide on a date, time, and place for the Ecology Festival. You may even want to create a logo, slogan, or cheer for this event. Create invitations using an environmental design or symbol and use recycled paper in its production such as paper bags, old wrapping paper, or old newspaper.

2. **DRESS OR COSTUMES:** Encourage guests to dress in "green" or to create costumes such as hand-painted tee shirts and party hats based on an ecological theme.

3. **DECORATIONS:** Create wind socks, flags, or computer-generated banners featuring elements of nature or the environment. Make leaf or flower prints, strings of popcorn or berries, and pet rocks or pine cone creatures to decorate your festival site. Stage a door decorating contest for other classrooms in your school and give awards to the "most beautiful door" featuring an ecological theme.

4. **EXHIBITS:** Encourage class members to work in pairs or small groups to create an exhibit in which to share information about the environment. Each exhibit should contain artifacts, posters, booklets, hand-outs, and displays based on a central environmental theme.

5. **PROGRAMS:** Prepare creative programs for the guests that outline the festival's events and sponsors. Include ecology puzzles, jokes, riddles, or stories for guests to enjoy.

6. **SPECIAL ACTIVITIES OR EVENTS:** Prepare a number of games and contests for guests to play. You may want to try revising versions of many traditional games such as Ecology Concentration (card game), Nature Jeopardy (TV game), or Pin the Leaf on the Tree (blindfold game).

7. **EVALUATION:** Design an evaluation form in the shape of a leaf or a flower that asks the guests to give you feedback on the success of your festival. Use these to create a king-size bulletin board as a reminder of your big day.

A DAY IN THE LIFE OF A WORKER

DIRECTIONS:

Select a specific job role or career that is of special interest to you. Research the career to find out everything you can about it. Consider such job elements as hours, salary and benefits, personal rewards and satisfaction, importance to society, types of skills required, special education or training required, potential for advancement, typical activities and tasks associated with job, future relevance of job, and creativity associated with job.

Use the time line below to report and record the findings from your research. Do this by writing in typical job roles, responsibilities, and responses for each time slot. Be prepared to present your time line to the class using some audiovisual aid or prompt.

7:00 a.m. _____

8:00 a.m. _____

9:00 a.m. _____

10:00 a.m. _____

11:00 a.m. _____

12:00 p.m. _____

1:00 p.m. _____

2:00 p.m. _____

3:00 p.m. _____

4:00 p.m. _____

5:00 p.m. _____

6:00 p.m. _____

7:00 p.m. _____

8:00 p.m. _____

9:00 p.m. _____

10:00 p.m. _____

Name_____ Date _____

PARTICIPATING IN A JURY TRIAL

DIRECTIONS:

It takes many talented and well-trained people to prepare for and participate in a jury trial. One way to give students practice in a mock court of law is to have them simulate a trial using a case with which they are familiar and can complete in a reasonable period of time. Popular fairy tales work well for this purpose.

Work with a small group of students to prepare for a mock trial using a fairy tale of interest to the entire group. Consider such stories as "Cinderella," "Sleeping Beauty," "Jack and the Beanstalk," "Little Red Riding Hood," or "Snow White and the Seven Dwarfs." To begin this project, carefully read the story you have chosen to use as the basis of your trial. Determine who the major characters will be, using the roles outlined below. Assign the various roles to members of your group and have each group member write a "role card" to use in carrying out his or her job description and performance during the trial. Decide what the charges will be ahead of time and establish the ground rules for this simulation. Stage the trial before an audience and have classmates rate each of your performances using a rubric the group has created for this activity.

ROLES OF AND RESPONSIBILITIES FOR THE MOCK TRIAL

1. **Judge:**
   The judge presides over the trial and reads the charges to the defendant in his or her opening remarks. The judge also rules on the objections by the attorneys, allows for re-examination of the witnesses, gives instructions to the jury, and administers the sentence to the defendant if there is one. Common expressions the judge will use in his or her role are:
   a. You are charged with . . .
   b. If convicted you will . . .
   c. How do you plead?
   d. Objection sustained.
   e. Objection overruled.

2. **Defendant:**
   The defendant is the person accused of the crime. The defendant is always innocent until proven guilty.

3. **Defense Attorney:**

   The defense attorney, along with the prosecuting attorney, selects the jury members and also attempts to show that no crime has been committed by the defendant. The defense attorney makes an opening statement to support his or her case as well as a closing argument to summarize his or her position. The defense attorney also cross-examines the witnesses and prepares the case arguments.

4. **Prosecutor or Prosecuting Attorney:**

   The prosecutor, along with the defense attorney, selects the jury members and also tries to show that a crime has been committed by the defendant. The prosecutor makes an opening statement to support his or her case as well as a closing argument to summarize his or her position. The prosecutor always starts first because the prosecution has the burden of proving the guilt of the defendant. The prosecutor also examines the witnesses before the defense attorney is allowed to cross-examine the witnesses.

5. **Court Recorder:**

   The court recorder makes an exact transcript of every word spoken during the proceedings of the trial using a "stenotype" machine. During your trial, however, the court recorder will probably only be able to take notes that approximate the proceedings of the trial.

6. **Bailiff:**

   The bailiff "swears in" the witnesses and instructs the observers in the courtroom to rise or be seated when the judge and jury enter and leave the courtroom. Common expressions the bailiff will use in this role are:

   a. Please raise your right hand. Do you solemnly swear to tell the truth, the whole truth, and nothing but the truth, so help you God?

   b. Please rise. Please be seated.

   c. All rise. District Court for the City of _____, the Honorable Judge _____ (name) presiding, is now in session.

7. **Witnesses for the Prosecution and Defense:**

   Witnesses for the prosecution and defense are individuals selected by the defense attorney or the prosecutor to provide evidence of the defendant's guilt or lack of guilt through testimony.

8. **Jury Members:**

   Members of the jury are mutually interviewed and appointed by both the defense attorney and the prosecutor respectively. It is important that potential jury members display no bias toward the defendant or his or her crime.

MAKE IT A DEBATABLE PERFORMANCE

DIRECTIONS:

A debate is a formal discussion with specific rules for its participants. Members of a debate team must agree on a topic, question, issue, or resolution that is to be researched, clarified, and debated. There are two sides to a debate—an affirmative side that argues in favor of the resolution and a negative side that argues against the resolution. The debate process is one that takes place in a controlled setting through structured controversy. The winner of the debate is determined by a panel of judges who make their decision based on the quality of research and the reasonableness of the arguments presented by each side. Every debate also has a timekeeper who presides over the debate process and a moderator who enforces the rules.

To stage a debate, students must decide on a topic or resolution on which to argue. Once this decision is made, four students elect to argue for the affirmative side of the resolution and four students elect to argue for the negative side of the resolution. Both sides spend considerable time researching the topic and compiling evidence for their respective positions. On the day of the debate, a large table is placed at the front of the room. The moderator is seated in the middle of the table, the teams are positioned on the ends of the table, the timekeeper is off to the side of the table, and the judges are seated in front of the table. The moderator introduces the resolution and the team members, reviews the rules, and officially begins the debate. The rules for conducting the debate may vary from group to group; one successful debate format is outlined on page 115.

Some possible topics for you to consider are:

- Year-round Schools
- School Choice for Parents
- Inclusion of all Special Education Students in Mainstreamed Classrooms, Regardless of Handicap
- Free Health Care for all Americans
- Government Shelters for the Homeless
- Schools without Walls
- Mandatory Community Service for High School Graduation
- Alternative or Magnet Schools in Every District

Work with a group of students in your class to plan and prepare for a debate on a resolution of your choice. Develop a rubric for the judges to use in selecting the winning side of your debate. What criteria should they use in making their decision?

RULES FOR A 25-MINUTE DEBATE

	Time	What
1.	3 minutes	First Speaker for the affirmative makes opening statement.
2.	3 minutes	First Speaker for the negative makes opening statement. (No questions or interruptions allowed during these times.)
3.	3 minutes	Second and Third Speakers for the affirmative stand and are questioned by the Second and Third Speakers for the negative. They answer as best they can.
4.	3 minutes	Second and Third Speakers reverse roles. The affirmative side questions, and the negative side answers.
5.	5 minutes	Recess for both sides to discuss closing ideas with final speakers.
6.	2 minutes	Fourth Speaker for the affirmative side summarizes.
7.	2 minutes	Fourth Speaker for the negative side summarizes.
8.	4 minutes	Judges withdraw to determine the winner of the debate.

ENGAGING IN A MAJOR PERFORMANCE ACTIVITY

DIRECTIONS:

You are the inventor of a new product that will soon be sold in stores across the country. It is your job to assist the president of a major advertising firm in marketing this product on a national basis. To meet this challenge, you must successfully perform the following tasks.

1. INVENT THE PRODUCT
   a. Explain what the product does and how it works.
   b. Explain what the product looks like and how it was invented.
   c. Explain what the product will be called and who is most likely to buy it.
   d. Explain what types of stores are most likely to carry it and what types of competitive products are most likely to be affected by it.

2. DESIGN THE PACKAGE
   a. Create a package, label, and warranty for your new product.
   b. Make certain that the package is the right size, shape, and color for the product and that it is accurate and informative.
   c. Make certain that the package makes people want to buy this product instead of something similar or competitive.

3. TRAIN A SALES FORCE
   a. Develop a script that a group of sales representatives will use to convince store managers to stock and sell the new product.
   b. Outline a product demonstration to present at a meeting with these potential store managers.

4. DEVELOP A RADIO OR TELEVISION COMMERCIAL
Plan and produce a commercial to advertise the new product on either a popular radio or television station. Make certain that the commercial is compatible with the type of show that it will sponsor. Consider such shows as sitcoms, adventure/mystery shows, talk shows, news shows, or musical variety shows.

5. CREATE A MAGAZINE OR NEWSPAPER AD
Create a one-page ad for a magazine or a one-fourth-page ad for a newspaper. Make certain that your ad design reflects the theme of the magazine or the section of the newspaper in which it will appear.

A NO-FAIL STUDENT CHECKLIST FOR DEVELOPING A PERFORMANCE PROJECT

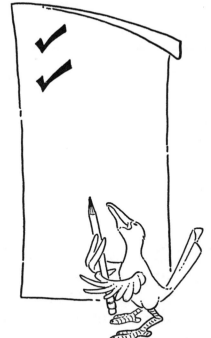

1. My title is meaningful and of interest to me.

2. The topic or theme I have selected is one that meets the approval of my teacher and relates to our required curriculum.

3. I have sources readily available to complete the project according to plan.

4. With my teacher's help, I have established a realistic timetable for developing and presenting my final performance.

5. I will be able to field-test or receive input as needed from my classmates and teacher.

6. My teacher and I are in agreement on a final response format for my performance as well as the overall learning goals I am expected to accomplish.

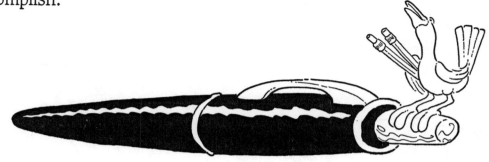

Name _____ Date _____

THREE UNIQUE PERFORMANCE ASSESSMENT MEASURES TO TRY

DIRECTIONS:

Review the following strategies for using performance assessment measures in your classroom and create or locate a springboard that could be used to introduce each strategy to your students.

STRATEGY ONE:
R AND R GROUPS
(RESPONSE AND REACTION GROUPS)

Divide the class into small cooperative learning groups. Give each group the same springboard to use for this activity. The springboard can take many forms (a photograph, quotation, tape recording, newspaper article, poster, etc.) but should focus on a controversial topic or issue. Ask each group to analyze, hypothesize, and synthesize information about the springboard item through discussion and interaction. Then, instruct each group to prepare a group response and reaction to the item, and tell them to be prepared to give this group report to the rest of the class.

ADVANTAGES OF THIS GROUP PERFORMANCE FOR STUDENTS:

1. It increases student interaction and involvement with the topic and with one another.
2. It significantly increases student response time.
3. It engages students reluctant to contribute to a large group discussion.
4. It encourages collaborative problem-solving.
5. It focuses discussion on student-generated ideas rather than teacher-generated ideas.

STRATEGY TWO:

ACTING OUT EVENTS THROUGH SCENARIOS

Divide the class into small groups and give each group a photograph, illustration, slide, or drawing of a significant event to use as a springboard in the subject area being studied. Allow time for the groups to study the item and think critically about it. Then, instruct the students to organize themselves and to physically assume the positions and roles of the characters in the photograph, illustration, slide, or drawing. Encourage the groups to create a "live mini-drama" suggested by the springboard, depicting actual scenes and dialogue of realistic actions and behaviors that might have occurred before, during, and after this setting. The group is to act out and portray any possible events or situations connected with the springboard.

STRATEGY THREE:

LIVING PICTURES

Give each student a picture or photograph that is related in some way to the topic or subject area being studied. The student's task is to create a set of six questions to accompany each picture or photograph—one for each level of Bloom's Taxonomy. Have the student use the picture or photograph to answer the questions and prepare a short oral interpretation of the situation being portrayed in the springboard item.

A COOPERATIVE LEARNING GROUP PERFORMANCE

DIRECTIONS:

Work in cooperative learning groups of four. Make certain that each group member has one of the following jobs: Recorder (secretary for the group); Facilitator (chairperson for the group); Timekeeper (taskmaster for the group); and Materials Manager (gopher for the group).

Your job is to select a novel or other book of fiction for each member of the group to read individually and discuss collectively. Then, select one of the activities outlined below to use as a springboard for sharing your book with other students in the class. All members of your group must be actively engaged in the "book-sharing" performance.

Upon completion of your activity, have each group member complete the rubric on the next page. Use this as a basis for discussing how well you performed as a group to complete this task.

ACTIVITY OPTION ONE: A Panel Presentation

Each member of your group becomes the group expert and spokesperson in one of the following areas: characters, theme, setting, and plot. Each member gives a summary of his or her area in a formal panel presentation before the class.

ACTIVITY OPTION TWO: A News Broadcast

Each member in your group becomes a partner of a news team for your local television station. Each person selects favorite and representative passages and events from the book to report on and take turns giving a brief but newsworthy accounting of the situation before the rest of the students.

ACTIVITY OPTION THREE: A Quiz Show

One member of your group becomes the host of a popular quiz show and the other three members become quiz show contestants competing for a prize. Questions from the book are posed to the contestants by the host according to a procedure established by the group. A winner is selected and a prize is awarded.

RUBRIC: COOPERATIVE LEARNING GROUP PERFORMANCE

DIRECTIONS:

Review the steps you completed to plan, prepare, and deliver your book-sharing presentation. Complete each of the statements below to analyze how well the members of your group worked together. Select the most appropriate rating for each area and be able to defend your decision to other members of the group.

RATING SCALE:

3 = SUPER   2 = SATISFACTORY   1 = NEEDS IMPROVEMENT

_____1. Each member of our group handled his or her group role.

_____2. Each member of our group took turns listening to one another's ideas.

_____3. Each member of our group actively engaged in the assigned learning task.

_____4. Each member of our group applied his or her conflict resolution skills when appropriate to do so.

_____5. Each member of our group showed respect for one another.

_____6. Each member of our group made a major contribution to the overall performance.

_____7. Each member of our group displayed a sense of humor.

_____8. Each member of our group seemed to enjoy the assignment.

SUMMARY:

If I were the teacher and the audience of this performance, I would give our group a(n) ___ (letter grade) because _____

_____

_____

_____

_____

_____

_____

Name _____ Date _____

PERSONAL REFLECTIONS
ABOUT MY PERFORMANCE

DIRECTIONS:

Make a working outline (for your own use only) of how you planned and carried out the preparation and presentation of your performance. Reflect on the outline and try to assess the degree of success of each step as well as of the overall experience. Think about what you consider to be the high points and what you would do differently next time. Ask yourself such questions as:

(1) What did I really learn from this experience?

(2) Could I have used my time more productively by writing a report, carrying out a research project, studying for a test, or completing some other traditional activity?

(3) What tasks were most challenging, most interesting, and most beneficial for me?

(4) Would I recommend performance assessment to my teacher as an ongoing part of our classroom evaluation procedures?

After thoughtful reflection, use the space below to write an essay expressing your feelings and opinions about the value of Performance Assessment to students of your age. (You may need to continue your essay on a separate piece of paper.) Since you may decide to include this reflection in your portfolio, make it a clear, insightful representation of your feelings.

_____

_____

_____

_____

_____

_____

_____

_____

Name _____ Date _____

APPENDIX

USING AN INTERDISCIPLINARY UNIT TO MAKE PORTFOLIOS, PRODUCTS, AND PERFORMANCES MEANINGFUL AND MANAGEABLE

In recognizing and attempting to meet the needs of individual student learning styles within a group setting, teachers are finding the interdisciplinary unit to be an invaluable aid. The unit organization not only provides a framework for meaningful integration of subject matter, but also offers a wide variety of activities for students to make choices that best accommodate his or her own interests and learning styles.

When the unit is introduced, inform students that they will be required to select a portfolio artifact, a performance presentation, and a product to be used as assessment measures. This culminating activity will allow students and teachers to evaluate achievement and determine the overall success of the unit. Since they have participated in establishing and accepting responsibility for the criteria to be used in evaluation, students will plan and complete the individual activities with more enthusiasm, purpose, and commitment. Furthermore, the carefully developed interdisciplinary unit provides an excellent opportunity for creative integration of subject matter, student ownership in the entire learning process, and meaningful authentic assessment.

USING AN INTERDISCIPLINARY UNIT TO MAKE PORTFOLIOS, PRODUCTS, AND PERFORMANCES MEANINGFUL AND MANAGEABLE

Pencil Power is a model interdisciplinary unit with a generic theme that can be easily adapted for use with students in widely varying situations. The activities have been planned to be open-ended and of a general nature. This format provides teachers and students with a great deal of freedom, allowing them to tailor the activities to meet individual interests and needs. Reference materials and necessary supplies have been kept simple, and all should be readily available in most schools.

PENCIL POWER

AN INTERDISCIPLINARY UNIT TO ACCOMMODATE A VARIETY OF LEARNING STYLES

Verbal/Linguistic: Select one of the following creative writing assignments to complete:

1. Compose an ode to a pencil.
2. Write a story about a magic pencil that never misspelled a word.
3. Write a newspaper feature about a special project whose purpose is to provide an adequate supply of pencils for every student in every country of the world.
4. Compose a series of raps in praise of the frequently unappreciated yellow pencil.

Logical/Mathematical: Use your pencil to measure at least ten objects in your classroom. Record your findings on a chart.

Visual/Spatial: Draw an exact scale model of your pencil. Give attention to shape, dimensions, and special features.

Bodily/Kinesthetic: Balance your pencil on your finger. Then try using a variety of center points to balance one pencil on another or to balance a pencil on a ball point pen.

Musical/Rhythmic: Use your pencil to tap out a nursery rhyme or simple song on your desk. Experiment to find out which end of your pencil is most effective in achieving the desired tonal patterns and if a pencil with a very sharp point is preferable to a one with a blunt point. Record the pattern with a series of dots and dashes.

Interpersonal: Use a graph to display the results of a survey that you conduct with members of your class to determine the most popular pencil color for regular classroom use.

Intrapersonal: Use the phrase, "The pencil is mightier than the sword" as the subject of an essay focusing on human relations.

PENCIL POWER

BRAINSTORMING CHALLENGES

Challenge One: List three situations where a pencil with a red point would be preferable to an ordinary lead one.

Challenge Two: Tell two ways you could sharpen a pencil if you had neither a pencil sharpener nor a knife.

Challenge Three: Agree or disagree with the following statement. Support your position.
A leading pencil manufacturer recently expressed concern that the ordinary lead pencil may soon become obsolete.

Challenge Four: Find out and explain why China has historically been the world's leading producer of pencils.

Challenge Five: Use your pencil to point out a location on the world map that represents a place you would like to visit, then use your pencil to trace and record the pathway you would follow to reach that destination from your home. Determine the methods of transportation you would use and the approximate amount of time and money required for the trip.

Challenge Six: Make up a game entitled, "Spin the Pencil," "Pencil Password," "Pencil Relay," or "Pitch the Pencil, Please."

Challenge Seven: Compose an original play to portray the story of a humorous incident involving a missing pencil, a pencil made of gold, or a pencil that could not write a lie.

Challenge Eight: Compare and contrast one of the following:
    a pencil and a ball point pen
    a pencil and a watercolor brush
    a pencil and a stick of chalk
    a pencil and a crayon
Use a Venn diagram to show your findings.

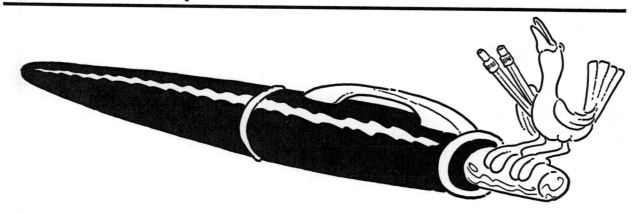

Challenge Nine: Outline the steps in the manufacturing and marketing of an ordinary lead pencil.

Challenge Ten: Design a special pencil to commemorate each of the following occasions:
    the dedication of a nature trail
    the centennial celebration of a public library
    a fundraiser to benefit homeless people

Challenge Eleven: Make a list of questions you would like to find answers to on a class field trip to a pencil factory.

Challenge Twelve: Develop an outline and plan for creating a class mural depicting the pencil industry, from the supply of raw materials to the availability of pencils in the marketplace.

LESSON PLAN TO ACCOMMODATE INDIVIDUAL DIFFERENCES IN LEARNING STYLES

DIRECTIONS:

Design your own "Pencil Power" lesson plan by selecting four of the seven activities listed on the Pencil Power Unit Overview. Reflect on your list of activities and choose three to five of the brainstorming challenges to reinforce and give balance to your study.

LEARNING ACTIVITIES:

1. _____
   _____
2. _____
   _____
3. _____
   _____
4. _____
   _____

BRAINSTORMING CHALLENGES:

1. Challenge _____
   _____
2. Challenge _____
   _____
3. Challenge _____
   _____
4. Challenge _____
   _____

PLAN FOR COMPLETION:

Date To Begin Study _____ Date To Complete Study_____

Materials Needed _____

Plan Of Action_____

Name _____ Date _____

SAMPLE ANECDOTAL RECORD FORM FOR TEACHER USE

Observations of students and maintenance of anecdotal records are helpful tools for teachers to use in the performance assessment process. Although there are many formats available for this purpose, the following Anecdotal Record Form is a simple, flexible model. It may be used as is or modified to meet your needs.

Student's Name _____   Observer's Name _____

Date _____   Subject _____

DESCRIPTION OF INSTRUCTIONAL SITUATION:

_____

_____

_____

_____

_____

_____

_____

_____

_____

DESCRIPTION OF INSTRUCTIONAL TASK:

_____

_____

_____

_____

_____

_____

_____

_____

BEHAVIORS/ACTIONS OBSERVED:

_____

_____

_____

_____

_____

_____

_____

IMPLICATIONS OF BEHAVIORS/ACTIONS OBSERVED:

_____

_____

_____

_____

_____

_____

_____

FOLLOW-UP SUGGESTIONS:

_____

_____

_____

_____

_____

_____

_____

_____

QUESTIONING STRATEGIES FOR LEADING A GROUP DISCUSSION

When conducting a group discussion, it is important to remember these guidelines for asking better questions. Use this checklist to help you prepare for leading a quality discussion on a topic of your choice.

1. Prepare your questions ahead of time, varying the types and levels of your questions. Use Bloom's Taxonomy to help you identify these levels.

2. Ask only one question at a time. Allow plenty of time after each question for the group to reflect on the meaning of the question and to formulate their answers.

3. State questions clearly and concisely before calling for responses.

4. Do not repeat your questions too readily, and do not repeat peer responses too quickly.

5. Encourage the group to direct their responses to one another and to question you, the leader, and each other when appropriate to do so.

6. Insist that each member of the group gives a complete answer to the question before moving to another topic.

7. Call on both males and females and those who volunteer and those who do not, so that there is a balance in your questioning plan.

8. Provide meaningful hints or assistance to those who supply incorrect responses to a discussion question.

CHARACTERISTICS OF THE NEW ASSESSMENT MODELS

DIRECTIONS:

Read through the list of characteristics of the new assessment models being used in many schools today. Place an asterisk (*) next to each characteristic that makes sense to you as a teacher and/or as a student. Be ready to discuss reasons for your responses.

_____ 1. What we teach or learn (the curriculum) and how we teach or learn (the instruction) should drive how we measure achievement (the assessment).

_____ 2. Standardized tests are limited in their application because there are no "standard" students.

_____ 3. Student portfolios, performances, and products provide a more holistic picture of a student's progress than paper-and-pencil tests.

_____ 4. Because the learning process is as important as the content to be learned, alternative assessment tools and techniques are required.

_____ 5. The knowledge "explosion" has made it impossible to learn everything in a given subject area, so it becomes more important to teach students how to learn, how to think, and how to design assessment measures accordingly.

_____ 6. The student prefers active learning situations over passive learning situations (including the testing process).

_____ 7. Students vary in their intellectual development and, as a result, testing must be individualized and developmentally appropriate.

_____ 8. Assessment should be used to diagnose each student's needs rather than to compare and rank students against one another.

_____ 9. Although authentic assessment measures take more time to administer and score, they are preferable to standardized and/or objective tests.

_____ 10. Students have a right to know what is to be tested before assessment takes place.

MYTHS ABOUT TESTING
THAT YOU NEED TO THINK ABOUT

DIRECTIONS:

Think about all of the standardized tests, textbook quizzes, and subject area exams that you have administered over the past several years. Give at least one detailed example from your personal experience that negates each of the testing myths outlined below.

MYTH ONE:
STUDENTS LEARN BEST BY IMITATION AND MEMORIZATION.

_____

_____

_____

_____

_____

_____

_____

_____

_____

_____

MYTH TWO:
THERE IS USUALLY A SINGLE RIGHT ANSWER TO A TEST QUESTION OR PROBLEM.

_____

_____

_____

_____

_____

_____

_____

_____

_____

MYTH THREE:
TESTS SHOW WHAT A STUDENT KNOWS OR DOES NOT KNOW.

_____

_____

_____

_____

_____

_____

MYTH FOUR:
OBJECTIVE TESTS ARE THE BEST WAY TO MEASURE
THE MOST IMPORTANT IDEAS IN A GIVEN SUBJECT AREA.

_____

_____

_____

_____

_____

_____

MYTH FIVE:
IN THE CLASSROOM,
ONLY THE TEACHER CAN ADEQUATELY ASSESS A STUDENT'S PROGRESS.

_____

_____

_____

_____

_____

_____

USING LITERATURE SELECTIONS
TO MAKE PORTFOLIOS, PRODUCTS, AND PERFORMANCES
MEANINGFUL AND MANAGEABLE

Literature selections of high interest to students can be used in many creative ways to stimulate interest in classroom discussions, to encourage use of higher order thinking skills, to provide the basis for process and creative writing assignments, and, of course, to develop and enrich reading skills and appreciation. As a by-product of literature-related activities, portfolio artifacts, product exhibits, and performance presentations may be built into lesson plans and project outlines. Book-related projects such as reference and research papers, book reports, dramatic performances, murals, dioramas, and art projects may all be used for authentic assessment purposes when the criteria for evaluation has been carefully planned and made clear to students from the onset of the project.

USING LITERATURE SELECTIONS
TO MAKE PORTFOLIOS, PRODUCTS, AND PERFORMANCES
MEANINGFUL AND MANAGEABLE

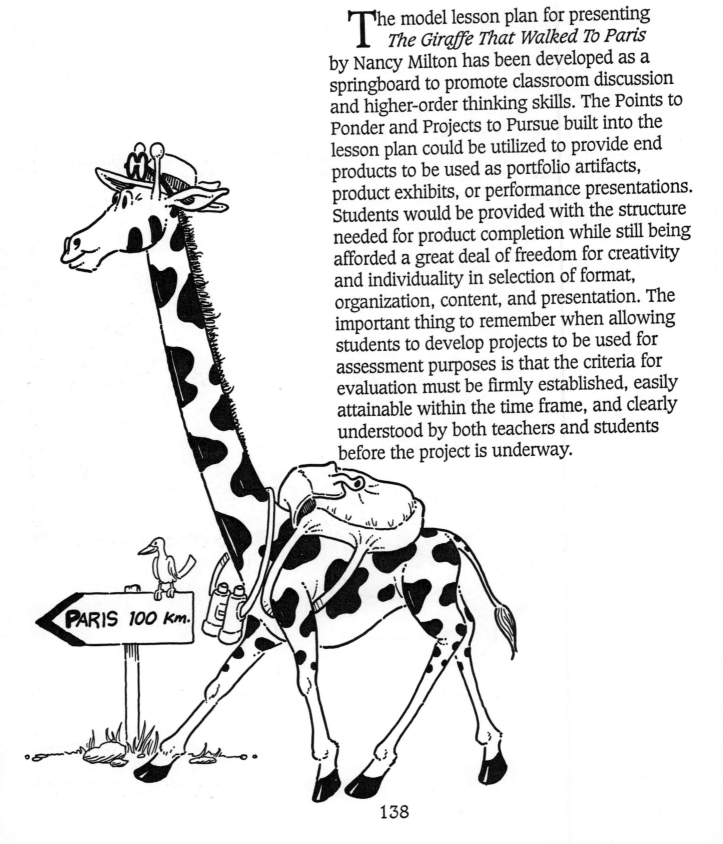

The model lesson plan for presenting *The Giraffe That Walked To Paris* by Nancy Milton has been developed as a springboard to promote classroom discussion and higher-order thinking skills. The Points to Ponder and Projects to Pursue built into the lesson plan could be utilized to provide end products to be used as portfolio artifacts, product exhibits, or performance presentations. Students would be provided with the structure needed for product completion while still being afforded a great deal of freedom for creativity and individuality in selection of format, organization, content, and presentation. The important thing to remember when allowing students to develop projects to be used for assessment purposes is that the criteria for evaluation must be firmly established, easily attainable within the time frame, and clearly understood by both teachers and students before the project is underway.

PARIS 100 Km.

LITERATURE SPRINGBOARDS

TOPIC: Geography and History — Paris, France

BOOK TITLE: *The Giraffe That Walked To Paris*

AUTHOR: Nancy Milton

ILLUSTRATOR: Roger Roth

PUBLISHER: Crown Publishers, Inc.,
New York, 1992

SYNOPSIS: This is the true story of the first giraffe ever to live in Europe thanks to the pasha of Egypt who decided to give her as a gift to the King of France in 1826. The giraffe travels to Marseilles, then through the towns and villages of France all the way to Paris. The story celebrates the giraffe's arrival in the capital where she receives many visitors, accolades, and souvenirs to commemorate the event.

POINTS TO PONDER:

1. Summarize the real events, real people, and real places that are used as the historical basis for the story.

2. How would you describe the illustrations in this book, and how do they convey a sense of the history and culture of the times?

3. How would you describe the personality of La Girafe?

4. Decide whether you would have wanted to attend the celebration of La Girafe's entrance into Paris or not. Give reasons for your choice.

Projects To Pursue:

1. Pretend that you are to visit the city of Paris for two weeks this summer. Develop an itinerary of where you would want to go and what you would want to see.

2. Research information about giraffes and construct a fact sheet about their habits and natural habitats.

3. Locate the countries of Egypt and France on a globe or map. Determine the easiest route from Alexandria, Egypt, to Paris, France. Draw a map showing this route.

4. Locate passages in the story that display the author's sense of humor. Select one passage to illustrate with your creative interpretation of the author's sense of humor.

AN ANNOTATED BIBLIOGRAPHY OF INCENTIVE PUBLICATIONS TITLES
Selected To Provide Additional Help For Making
Portfolios, Products, And Performances Meaningful And Manageable
For Students And Teachers

Cook, Shirley. *180 Days Around the World.* Nashville, TN: Incentive Publications, 1993. (Grades 4-8)
This resource contains a series of global challenges that send students on an adventure around the world and provide them with clever opportunities to discuss, research, think, imagine, and explore.

___. *Story Journal for Middle Grades.* Nashville, TN: Incentive Publications, 1990. (Grades 4-8)
These seventeen literature selections are organized around familiar high-interest topics and offer meaningful ways of presenting new vocabulary and stimulating creative responses through collaborative discussions and daily journal-writing activities.

Farnette, Cherrie, Imogene Forte, and Barbara Loss. *I've Got Me and I'm Glad, Revised Edition.* Nashville, TN: Incentive Publications, 1989. (Grades 4-7)
A self-awareness resource with high-interest reproducible activities designed to help kids identify their strengths and weaknesses and establish both short- and long-range goals.

___. *People Need Each Other, Revised Edition.* Nashville, TN: Incentive Publications, 1989. (Grades 4-7)
This collection of social-awareness activities was designed to build student understanding of family, peers, and the community by encouraging the use of effective communication skills.

Forte, Imogene. *Reading Survival Skills for the Middle Grades.* Nashville, TN: Incentive Publications, 1994. (Grades 5-8)
Prepare students for tomorrow's world with these exercises and activities developed to improve reading proficiency and language acquisition, integrate reading, writing, thinking, and speaking skills, and connect reading to real-life experiences.

Forte, Imogene and Joy MacKenzie. *Writing Survival Skills for the Middle Grades.* Nashville, TN: Incentive Publications, 1991. (Grades 5-8)
Test-taking, resumes, business letters, and job applications are only a few of the topics covered in the student pages and teacher-directed sections of this essential writing skills handbook.

Forte, Imogene and Sandra Schurr. *The Definitive Middle School Guide: A Handbook for Success.* Nashville, TN: Incentive Publications, 1993. (Grades 5-8)
This comprehensive, research-based manual provides the perfect overview for educators and administrators who are determined to establish a school environment that stimulates and motivates the Middle Grade student in the learning process.

___. *Interdisciplinary Units and Projects for Thematic Instruction for Middle Grade Success.* Nashville, TN: Incentive Publications, 1994. (Grades 5-8)
A jumbo-size collection of thematic-based interdisciplinary activities and assignments that was created to spark interest, encourage communication, and promote problem-solving as well as decision-making.

___. *Tools, Treasures, and Measures for Middle Grade Success.* Nashville, TN: Incentive Publications, 1994. (Grades 5-8)
A wide assortment of teaching essentials, from ready-to-use lesson plans and student assignments to valuable lists and assessment tools, have been assembled in this practical resource.

Frank, Marge. *If You're Trying To Teach Kids How To Write, You've Gotta Have This Book, Revised Edition.* Nashville, TN: Incentive Publications, 1995. (All grades)
The new and improved version of this already popular book is filled with creative ideas and activities to motivate all students to want to write. It has been updated with current information on using portfolios, assessing student learning, and encouraging students to revise and edit their work.

___. *Using Writing Portfolios To Enhance Instruction and Assessment.* Nashville, TN: Incentive Publications, 1994. (All grades)
This comprehensive reference offers specific guidelines and detailed approaches on how to best manage and use student portfolios as instructional and assessment tools.

Frender, Gloria. *Learning To Learn.* Nashville, TN: Incentive Publications, 1990. (All grades)
This comprehensive reference book is filled with creative ideas, practical suggestions, and "hands on" materials to help students acquire the organizational, study, test-taking, and problem-solving skills they will need to become lifelong effective learners.

___. *Teaching for Learning Success: Practical Strategies and Materials for Everyday Use.* Nashville, TN: Incentive Publications, 1994. **(All grades)**
This ready-to-use resource guide has the materials needed to successfully implement cooperative learning techniques, organize and manage the classroom environment, adapt teaching to suit varied learning styles, and promote the home-school connection.

Graham, Leland and Daniel Ledbetter. *How To Write a Great Research Paper.* **Nashville, TN: Incentive Publications, 1994. (Grades 5-8)**
Simplify the research process by using mini-lessons to teach each step. Help students choose and narrow topics, locate appropriate information from a variety of sources, take notes, organize an outline, develop a rough draft, document sources, as well as write, revise, and evaluate their final papers.

Philpot, Jan and Ed. *Partners in Learning and Growing: Linking the Home, School, and Community Through Curriculum-Based Programs.* **Nashville, TN: Incentive Publications, 1994. (Grades 5-8)**
These original programs were designed to give a teacher or an entire school a year-long plan for fostering community and parental involvement.